Speckled Prism

Enriqueta Mayuga

Copyright © 2016 by Enriqueta Mayuga. 740705

ISBN:	Softcover	978-1-5144-8589-7
	Hardcover	978-1-5144-8590-3
	EBook	978-1-5144-8588-0

All rights reserved. No part of this book may be reproduced or transmitted in any form or by any means, electronic or mechanical, including photocopying, recording, or by any information storage and retrieval system, without permission in writing from the copyright owner.

Print information available on the last page

Rev. date: 06/06/2016

To order additional copies of this book, contact:
Xlibris
1-888-795-4274
www.Xlibris.com
Orders@Xlibris.com

Other Books Written By Author:
- Immigrant at Peace
- Spring, Autumn, Sunset
- Outspoken and Mute – American Life
- Splintered Dreams, Blades of Truth, Shafts of Sunlight
- Landscape of a Challenged Life

Dedication

To my mother - **Rosario Villacorta Vendivil**

To my father - **Joaquin Virtucio Cartagena**

......They gave more than they received

Contents

Dedication 1

Acknowledgement 5

Introduction: Speckled Prism 6

Review 7

About the Author 8

SECTION ONE
American Experience

America Is Not For All 10

New York Revisited 11

Murmurings Of A Transplant 15

A Mother's Testament to Her Children 18

Outrage At 26, Accepting At 62 20

The Village of my Pain – The Valley of my Joy 22

SECTION TWO
Smatterings of Life – Poetry

Just When 26

From Both Sides Now 27

But It Hurts As Much 28

We Become Who We Are 30

Reckoning	31
Ain't We All?	32
Forgiving the Enemy	33
The Yang Minus The Ying (In His Genome?)	34

SECTION THREE

Staples of the Soul – Essays

Blue Moon and Kosovo	36
Efecto (Inventory)	38
The Bottom Line	40
Those Restless Years – Never Too Late To Ruminate	41
Soul In Ice	43
Staying With The Fundamentals	45
Living On The Fringes	46
Staying The Course	48
Exploring The Tango Of Life	49

SECTION FOUR

The Lighter Side of Life

Big Sem - My Kind Of Dude	52
I Did It My Way	53
Am Ready For The Bloom	54
And People Think I Am Normal	55
When I'm Gone	56
The Manchild of Your Yearnings	58
Romance Comes Late To My Life	59

Acknowledgement

I am very grateful to Elizabeth Tan – erstwhile transcriptionist, talented artist and loyal friend. As true in my two books, **"Splintered Dreams, Blades of Truth, Shafts of Sunlight"** and **"Landscape of a Challenged Life",** she is proficient and talented – the ultimate professional. She will always be a part of my literary journey.

Natalie Safford, a newly minted English major, who recently graduated with honors at Gonzaga University, entered the picture when I thought my book was almost ready. Her insights are refreshing and enlightening. I followed all her tips to the latter. I am very grateful for the refinements. Thank you Roxanne Wokajance for being my literary confidant, and to Myla Din for always being there as my facilitator. Agnes Saquilayan and Argelio Tobar entered my life, in time, to provide the technological know-how. They worked on the visuals and formatted it so it will be ready for my publisher. I thank my beloved grandchild, Sofia, my Girl Friday – she will always be my term of endearment.

I am deeply endebted to Father Charles Skok, who is the literary fire behind my writing. He did a review on each of my five books and wrote the Preface on four of them starting my second book, **"Spring, Autumn and Sunset",** published in 2000. I admire his intellect, his theological and philosophical perspective; he is the literary catalyst for me. No acknowledgement is complete without mentioning the editor of my first five books, Tanya Sorenson Becker. She started me in 1997, believing that I have a literary seed that could spout. Thank you my dearest friend, Tanya. I thank Xlibris, my publisher.

Introduction: Speckled Prism

In writing this book, it is not my intention to reignite the searing pain that encrusted my wearied soul in a sad chapter of my life. If my previous writings were the unleashing and the imploding of my anguish in my earlier years in America, this book is all about closure.

Speckled Prism, my sixth book, shares similar format with my first book, *Immigrant at Peace*, published in 1997. Both are compilations of essays, short stories and poetry. My first book had its starting point in 1963 when I arrived as a medical intern in this country and felt emotionally slammed. It was a time when as a foreign, ethnic female physician in a male dominated health field, I felt unwelcomed by a society unprepared for my kind. Since then, a stretch of 53 years, I have amassed enough wins and losses - with hopes denied and redeemed, faith diminished and regained in a life both sundrenched and rain drenched. The two subsequent books of poems and prose, which followed were a continuum of my rage on racism, discrimination and injustice. Often marginalized and rejected by superiors and colleagues with shaggy values, I was embittered and enraged.

My fourth book, "*Splintered Dreams, Blades of Truth, Shaft of Sunlight*", published in 2011 intoned acceptance and forgiveness. In that book, I wrote in the poem titled, "*I Know My Place.*" It goes: "I know my place, / I refuse to peg my life with material space, / these false sanctuaries." I continued: "only rejection awaits me / condescending glance of the ill-informed, / from the half-baked / from charred souls". This book won an award in the Southwest Festival Authors competition. In my last book published in 2013 – "*Landscape of a Challenged Life*" which also won a book award, Reverend Father Skok who also did the preface wrote: "There is sadness in many of Dr. Mayuga's writings as there is sadness in life, / there is disappointment and pain, humiliation and degradation and above all, the sensitivity of a woman who cares and love whether she is praised or belittled". In the same book, I also wrote: "I do not feel myself as a victim but rather a casualty of unenlightened men, stunted in their ethos / unable to accept novelty and diversity / who find ethnicity, unwieldy, divisive, if not repugnant", (*At 69 – Beyond the Enfeebling Past*).

This present book, my sixth book, written eighteen years after my first book is an attempt of closure – the final exculpation of my past journey of pain. This book is divided into four chapters. It begins in chapter one: American Experience. I consider two of my writings here, "*A Mother's Testament to Her Children*" and "*The Village of my Pain, the Valley of my Hope*" as the *sine qua non* of my early American experience. All the essays in chapter three, *Staples of the Soul*, have never been published before and mostly written in the last 1-2 years but for a few that were written a few years back but only completed now. Two are definitely historically dated (*Blue Moon and Kosovo and Soul In Ice*). They are included because similar bloody upheavals from ideologic turmoil and political enmities sadly holds true in many other countries today.

Some of the essays are more commentaries on reality as I see it. This is a book of conjectures and questions rather than answers. It also includes short stories of my pre-war experience as a child growing up in the Philippines and disparate subjects. Except for a few poems from previous writings, the poems included have been written in the last one to two years.

The discernment of a woman long past her prime differs from that of an infuriated, aggrieved and maligned youthful idealist. Long past the gory battlefield of survival, I now see the reality as a maze of honeycomb, fleeting spotlights, undulating shadows and occasional rainbows through my *speckled prism*.

Enriqueta C. Mayuga

Review

Speckled Prism is the sixth (and she says "final") book of Enriqueta Cartagena Mayuga, a medical doctor in Pasco, Washington. Her first book, published in 1997, was *Immigrant at Peace: A Woman Physician Reflects*. Dr. Mayuga asked me to offer some words of reflection on her words of reflection at that time. I did so, and for her next four books. Her words are far superior to mine.

Speckled Prism is a collection of both poetry and prose. I found it a fascinating book and read it in two sittings. There is a lyricism in her writing. The sharper edge of some of her earlier writing is now moderated by her acceptance of the reality of getting older, and the ensuing wisdom. The depth of feeling is still there, but there is a tinge of mellowness. She still expresses the sting of patronizing belittlement, but she moves beyond that in a somewhat uneasy acceptance of facts as facts.

One example is "Murmurings of a Transplant." She writes: "Inequities still sting but I am able to ferret / what I can do what is ideal." She has forgiven those who claim to be "the vanguard of equality," but they are *"unable to accept the nuances of / a culture they deem aberrant."* She adds: "Racism as known, has ceased to exist - / but its tentacles persist." She concludes: *"America is worth fighting for, / I do not know what others think - / but as for me - / I love America."*

Her writings have a poignancy, which express the core of her feelings and the candor of her soul.

Of her essays, I particularly enjoyed "Efecto (Inventory)." There is also pure joy in reading "The Bottom Line." "Staying with the Fundamentals" and "Living on the Fringes." There is a welcome bit of philosophical moralizing, and an expression of her strong faith in God. She writes in "The Bottom Line": *"We have to believe that our life on this planet is just one temporary step: a prelude to the next. Simply stated, we human beings have a soul, a God connection.* **This is incontrovertible – this is the bottom line**.*"*

"Those Restless Years – Never Too Late to Ruminate" shows the growing sense of unwelcome hopelessness gnawing at her soul. "I used to oppose with all my might and power the atrocities committed by men against his fellow human being," she wrote; but in later years, she notes, "I feel powerless about all the misdeeds and malfeasance before me and how little I can effect change." But she concludes: "My fellow human beings – do not judge me harshly because of this sense of detachment and helplessness. Wait till the last flaming tinder within me is squelched. Condemn me not, simply because I have lost my fire; sadly, **my soul is in ice**."

Chapter four is called "The Lighter Side of Life." It is lighter in the sense that comedy is not tragedy, but there is no frothy lightness. There are many thought-provoking lines. In "When I Am Gone," she is clear about the eulogy she does not want, but she concludes very seriously. "I bid adieu – so be at peace, / as I March to a forgiving land / where my secrets are safe / and no one would give a hoot about my skeletons, / and only the crosses I carried to meet my God / *are all that truly matter."*

Her final poem is *"Romance Comes Late to my Life."* The concluding stanza is "Children now grownups / - parents now gone, / and the calming waves that comes when / the battle is done./ *It is simply that I have found a new romance - / sizzling under each spell / of budding truth and serene thoughts / I am in love with life!"*

Speckled Prism is truly a delightful read.
Charles D. Skok, S.T.D., L.L.D.
Professor Emeritus of Religious Studies
Gonzaga University

About the Author

Enriqueta Cartagena Mayuga was born December 18, 1937 in the northernmost part of the Philippine Archipelago. Her father, a pioneering physician, moved his family to Cagayan Valley to serve as a medical director. Her mother, a pharmacist and a leading educator was an active community leader. Both parents had strong political and professional influence in the region.

She graduated from the University of Santo Tomas College of Medicine of 1962. The next year she came to the United States for medical training, which led her to New York, Kentucky and Texas. She completed her chief residency and Ob/Gyn fellowship at the University of Texas in San Antonio.

She started her medical practice n Pasco, Washington in 1970 and is the first female, foreign, Board Certified obstetrician-gynecologist in eastern Washington. At present, forty six years later, she still practices part-time Ob/Gyn in the Tri-Cities. Over the years, she has been active in various community affairs and also served as a State Board Advisory for Midwife and Nursing board. Her last stint was as a Board of Trustee for ten years at the Columbia Basin College in Pasco, Washington.

Her writings reflect her experiences as an immigrant, at the heights of the civil rights strifes; they also delve into her childhood experiences in Japanese-occupied Philippines, during World War II. She is published in nine different books of anthology in the United States and several publications – the last one: ***Field of Mirrors – An Anthology of Philippine American Writers.*** She also garnered special honors for her books, ***"Splintered Dreams, Blades of Truth, Shafts of Sunlight" and "Landscape of a Challenged Life",*** at the Southwest Festival of Authors competition. She is the author of five books of essays, prose poems and short stories. This book is her sixth book of essays and poems.

Enriqueta is the sibling of five and is married to Simeon Mayuga for 53 years. They have two children and five grandchildren and this summer of 2016 will mark her 53 years in America and 54 years as a medical physician.

Her books are available in Barnes and Noble, Xlibris and Amazon.

SECTION ONE

American Experience

"My children need not live my pain or rehash my emotional bondage".
From: **Outrage At 26, Accepting At 62**

America Is Not For All

Why did they think life is good
      -America is not for all,
The bastion of freedom lovers
        who want to make a go of life,
    past racial and social barricades
    past the bruising detour-
      into the verdant fields
        of opportunities.
America remains the Utopia of immigrants,
    -the Shangri-La for those willing
      to take the gauntlet
  -for those willing to plant and replant,
      where persistence is still the name of the game.

But America is not for the bleeding heart
    -nor for the meek, the tender or the naïve,
      the teetering and the wishy washy,
    -not for the imperfect, the quiet, the old,
      the impaired or the unhealthy,
      the onion skinned or the petrified soul,
It is a double-edged sword – a dichotomy,
    a paradise to many
    -a hell to some.

Enriqueta C. Mayuga

New York Revisited

Sagebrush in Idlewild
      awaited my arrival - a twenty hour flight,
It was the early 60's
      when groovy was the style
           no Hippies, no Yuppies then -
The 'Beat Generation'
      flower children - Delta Dawn song, prevailed
           Itinerant student I was -
                unheralded, unsought
                scurrying each summer
                chasing 'DSP's.
My New York was the four-cornered room
      where I worked and lived,
One year more training was my goal
      to keep the Feds from knocking at my door.

It seems so long ago
      my hospital now bulldozed to scraps -
A brand new institution now replaces it
      - unaware of my previous pain...
No more wall to keep me out
      no barbwire, immigration office to fear.
Hospital training was my microcosm
      the black and white divide was confounding me
My miscast group
      - a band of Asian Physician trainees
           unsure where we belong,
Harlem opened me to racial disparity
      a dichotomy I was unable to shake
My gratitude to Mother America
      while abhorring it's double standard
      caught me unprepared

    this social-cultural dislocation.
I never knew until then that I didn't fit
    the American medical and racial landscape,
      it is a bad dream, I felt
      a nightmare, which soon will pass.

The Vietnam War went on -
    my skills needed to replace
      physicians who went to the battlefield -
a trainee I was called, cheap labor
    and exploitations in actuality,
I would have been more likable
    if I closed my eyes to these -
Perhaps - a better training
    I could have had,
If only I could have bent and submitted
    to the hierarchical rules -
    but it was anathema to me
      to kowtow to these new oppressors
        (having come from a nation too long
      under colonialism).
So each summer, I wait nervously for the hospital DSP -
    afraid the Vietnam returnees
    will soon displace me at a moment's notice,
Without much ado, I will be dismissed
    under the guise of acceptable forms and rules
      of the contrived game,
      "It is legal - all documented,"
    so I understand, but it is hellish to have our backs
      continuously against the wall.

35 years later, I am back to New York
    now a mother of two
      New York and Texas born

    neither child aware
        this was my city of pain,
My son now living in New York directs me
    "Mom - remember it is the 'E' train
        not the 'F' train, then proceed to the 'A' train.
    Meekly, I submit and I comply
        more in fear of being lost
            in this subway I used to dread.
At each stop - I re-open my eyes
    hordes of riders with arms holding on to the rails
        more like glorified cattle
            civilly on their way to slaughter
But, their faces no longer terrorize me
Gone are the suspicious, condescending faces
    of long ago, when I was the only
        extraterrestrial creature (Filipino)
        in the subway of my fear.
Familiar faces now abound
    Asian, Latino, African, sprinkling of Caucasian.
    "Is this America?" I asked myself.
    "Am I dreaming? Is this outer space?"
Yesterday - a determined Chinese woman
    asked me, rather abruptly, for directions in Chinese
        (it could have been Yiddish!)
With no qualms I retorted,
    with Americanesque brusque
        half annoyed, half unsmiling,
    "Excuse me - I speak English only"
Then I thought, "My God,
    have I joined the Yankee hordes?"

Facing the Millennium,
    more mellowed I am,
    tolerant to pain,

    understanding the 'whys' of polarization
        but not embracing its enmity.

Circa, the millennium
    nobody has asked me yet - here in New York
        if I am an American or not.
Who is American?
    the SE Asians in Queens?
    the Afro-Americans in Harlem?
    the Puerto Ricans in Brooklyn?
    the Wall Street gazers at Bronxville?
    or Mayor Guiliani.

35 years ago
    I was an unknown
        beholden to the myth
    New York then aghast me
        Harlem broke my heart,
35 years later -
I am in a genuine state of beloved oblivion
    joyfully accepting my try,
        resigned to the dust of memories
            and my scrupulous dreams
    somewhat sullied by what lays before me:
        a polarized nation finding its soul,
        a plethora of what used to be unspeakable:
            bi-sexual, bi-racial, bipolar, live-ins.
'Marketability' displacing 'immutability'
    techno concepts, computer, Y2K, pre-occupation,
    even Jesus Christ - the Bible - in question,

America is still America, reluctant maybe -
    - it is the Land of the immigrant
New York is still New York
    and I am still me -
New York revisited
    - I needed to cleanse off the ghost
        which haunted me -
        men come and go
        but New York still is and will
        always be New York.
I do not mourn the New York of the past -
    not for a moment.

Enriqueta C. Mayuga

Murmurings Of A Transplant

I can afford to be sleeveless –
      I need nothing,
No hidden tattoo or indelible bruises,
Unafraid what lies beyond
      -I am at peace.
No biting tongue or furrowed mind can stifle me,
      I have taken the high road -
Long ago, I heralded my aspirations –
      as if sunrise was a sure thing,
I now lean back at my guide post –
      accept the gap between what I sought
      and what I have become,
Past my prime, chirping my style -
      old age attrition has finally unraveled.

Inequities still sting but I am able to ferret
      what I can do and what is ideal.
1970 is a mile stone -
      the first female ethnic obstetrician –
Little did I know I was treading no man's land,
      a brown bear in a polar artic world
At one point, my tormentors appeared to be winning,
I was the lightening rod of their discontent -
They trampled my rights -
      maimed my character
          unable to accept my intrusion
              in their jaded arena,
To them, my presence was anathema -
      Racist, avaricious competitors they were –
Their focus was to protect their economic franchise.

Today, I have stopped harping on past miscues,

  forgiven those who purports to be:
    the vanguard of equality -
Yet unable to accept the nuances of
  a culture they deem aberrant,
This was in the 60's – and limping through the 70's,
  with the black and white American divide,
And we, Asians, were caught in the middle -
  unsure of where we belong –
Perplexed by the poisonous fangs of discrimination -
  Ethnic Filipinos –were just a side show.
50 years later, we are now bonafide Americans –
  still passionate with our aspirations -
    in a sanctuary of literate zealots,
Religious strifes and oppression persist -
Not a day passes without turmoil and violence,
Religious fanatics continue to rock the earth -
Over 100 years past the Civil War –
  bestiality has returned in its worst form
  whether it be Isis or Boka Haram
Racial equality remains unsettled.

In the 60's, the black and white dispute reached a hilt,
  Lincoln's message was massaged -
    leaving seething questions of racism.
I came to America at the height of the Vietnam War -
  *F.M.G's we were called -
    Filling the slots of physician shortage.
Half a century has passed, changes have come -
  ambivalence have seeped through the nations core,
Spiritual emptiness abounds, ideologues on the rise,
Racism as known, has ceased to exist -
  but its tentacles persist,
Virtues pilloried - values shifted,

Today, the nation's character is at stake,

Materialism is the new religion

America is polarized

    -its values undermined

        -its people with contrasting prisms,

But those who are at the helm must lead,

    undo this decadence.

Cultural morass must be blunted –

    truth and equity the guiding light,

        America is worth fighting for,

I do not know what others may think –

But as for me -

    I love America.

(*F.M.G: Foreign Medical Graduates)

                                                  Enriqueta C. Mayuga

A Mother's Testament to Her Children

Out of the quicksand of life, I have emerged and survived – though bathed in mud. I have been bludgeoned, almost to a pulp, literally speaking, when the issues were strong and soul wrenching, dislodging me from my favored nest. Hindrances and roadblocks, I fought with tenacity and ferocity in my unflinching quest for social justice. Somehow, I was able to pick up the pieces, take charge and reverse my downslide. I learned a lot from those trying years. ***These are my thoughts as I look back at my nascent years in the America of the 60's when civil right laws were not in place.***

I realized that at times, there is no way to achieve one's goal, noble as it may be – much deserving as I felt. With meager resources, little time, and judicious patience, I got out of my entrapments – these moral and social prisons – "bloody but unbowed." At times, I had to bite the bullets, swallow the bitter pill of humiliation while I tried to extricate the embedded darts and poisoned arrows – but I prevailed. I stalled the force of misfortune, overcoming the wave of despair and discontent enabled by divine connection – horrified by the unwelcoming ambiance that I faced upon my entry to America. ***Prior to my coming here, I had no idea that the country was experiencing racial turmoil and there were undercurrent and prevailing prejudice on aliens who did not look or speak like the average citizenry. A Philippine passport did not exactly fit the ideal. This attitude also trickled down to the medical training programs where our presence was considered often times intrusive. At least we felt that way when confronted with put-down attitudes by more than a few of the hospital personnels.***

As I moved around my professional and business life, I began to better understand man in his own prism, his mastery of power and generational prejudices affecting his sights and judgments. ***Because of this, I transferred almost yearly to a new hospital training program – sometimes on my own volition and other times because my residency application was not renewed. It appears that the program director or the powers that select medical residents did not find me ideal. When I finally would get to a residency program, I was very cautious in how I conduct myself, afraid that my application for ascending residency might be rejected once again.*** Earlier in my medical training, I used to wonder why my fellow co-residents would manage an incongruous smile, a contrived laughter to humor the ego of those who held the power and mandate for our training contract. With no contract – there is no visa and thereby no medical training. The thought of being sacked from specialty training and being sent home (Philippines) as an illegal alien was a continuing sword of Damocles. I did not know how long I could endure another four years of training. The establishment, which hired us, was a mixed bag of good intentions and love for cheap labor. As resident physicians, we filled the needed help not only for training, but also for the hospital's miscellaneous technical and menial needs. Generally, the foreign medical graduates, as recipients of the Exchange Visitor's program, knew the rules and put up reasonably well with threats, both implied and overt. We knew that the American doctors who were conscripted for the Vietnam War will eventually come back and at any time, the hospitals will always find a "legitimate" way to boot us out. After all, we were only recruited from the Philippines and other countries to fill the temporary slot left by them. But then, I reminded myself that I came to this country on my own volition with a vibrant dream of my own. ***We were also aware that there were two sets of treatment for us foreign medical graduates and another for the native resident Americans – we, the interlopers, and they, the heir to the American***

Dream. At least that was our perception at the time. The consensus, even to the hot-tempered among us, was to play along – to co-exist, even though it meant submitting to the hierarchical bullies with their politics of coercion. ***When the highest authorities treated us well, the rest of the hierarchy down to the kitchen help and the house keepers also treated us well.*** We realized there was enough good in men and we needed to keep our judgment in abeyance. But with the ingrained cultural ignorance and racial intolerance, it was not uncommon to be addressed as "your people" – "your kind" – "your ways". Most of us felt victimized but then apartheid was worse and our own inner wranglings were after all, endurable.

For some of us reared up in a less docile upbringing, it was infuriating to see the pendulum constantly swinging before us. I kept reminding myself that the Hospital authorities had the power to discharge me and dislocate me (at that point I was still looking for the Promised Land). I could not tolerate, however, a few of my fellow trainees in their disingenuous and timorous ways. I was in a constant emotional upheaval; I could not afford to sit down in the theatre of contrived comfort and drink in the false aroma of contentment. Our stipend was a pittance, but still a manna in terms of the Philippine peso. Each time I thought of our dilemma I sulked, spewing ugly words from my once cautious tongue. As I neared the end of my specialty training, I moved to a different hospital and location so as not to be "enslaved" by the same institution. I also began to understand the language of forgiveness – even for those who look at me with disdain. While prejudice and injustice to ones fellow men was anathema to me, I felt there was a greater being, totally in charge, truly ubiquitous and could be palpable if I allowed Him to permeate me. ***After all, the suffering of Jesus makes our situation very miniscule. What if we are treated second or third class, Jesus was totally bludgeoned to death - deemed classless by his torturers.***

Thirty six years after I arrived here in America, I no longer dub the timid and the reticent as spineless. As much as I am enraged by academic and institutional blackmail, I have come to see it as the working politics of a Machiavellian inspired society. I no longer accuse the cowards of being mice, but I would still ferret out the mice from the men. As a practicing doctor, I am in another level of playing field. Racial discrimination, now illegal, still exists but is much subtle - its shadow permeating those who closed their eyes to injustice, education and humanity. Much progress has been achieved, but it is for our sons and daughters to be vigilant – ***not to allow its (racism) nucleus to resurface in the form of a backlash; not to allow the establishment and it's institutions to coat racism with bureaucratic mousetraps and contrived technical jargons.*** Like the now-abolished apartheid, the core of racism may have merely gone underground, half submerged and disguised by external societal niceties. Cosmetic and social engineering are very much evident; discrimination in some quarters still exists, though in many disguises, subtle and sub minimal.

It is circa 2013 – fifty years later since I came one sunny day in New York in June 1963 as a vibrant 26 year old. Today, I have a greater understanding of the nature of society. ***I know that there is a greater Hierarchy where the just prevails and God's angels are there for me.*** I now understand what true inner peace means – and what we need to believe and persevere in. At last the barricade of fear is removed – the wall of prejudice has been exposed, its sequelae transparent; the racial albatross is no longer a burden, but to the perpetrators. With serenity, I realize I have obtained the visa for all time. I truly believe that my passport to a ***more meaningful*** life is forthcoming.

Enriqueta C. Mayuga

Outrage At 26, Accepting At 62

Uncharted and clueless –
    spirited and newly minted,
Moonstruck at 26-
    this was the 60's,
To the rest of the world
    America was it!
But reality soon dashed my hopes
    and diminished my dreams,
I was baffled by a culture,
    fractious and intolerant,
Nonchalant to my flight,
I was an unwilling voice,
    forced to confront the social mien
    and double standard as it affected me
    and others treated with condescension.

Stilted by my pain-
    I didn't always see the light,
In constant fear of being deported,
    I felt I could never belong-
I bade goodbye so many times
    but couldn't muster the courage
    to return (to the Philippines)
        -broken and empty handed.
Failure was not an option-
Disgrace to the family was a
    fate worse than death,
I kept digging and probing
    unsure how long I could keep going
Alienated and dismayed
    by a clueless culture
    immersed in its own trivia.

I fought back
    unwilling to be society's pawn
I overstretched my reach
    beyond the restricted walls,
Interminable, my ordeal-
Stymied by emotional slivers
    I was close to the breaking point,
But recharged by faith, I set my focus,
America's eyes have opened,
    civil rights became the battle cry.

Today, the scraps of hope and
    garbs of faith have triumphed,
Equal opportunity is the law,
Inequity is not sanctioned
    (legally, at least).
Racism is being rectified.

A new generation, mixed and tolerant,
    suave and unshackled have emerged,
Our progenies now harvest the bounty
    of our toils and tears,
My children need not live my pain
    nor rehash my emotional bondage,
My grandchildren need not be
    of Mayflower descent,
Need not be boat children
    or aliens on the run-
    nor remain refugees for life,
They are simply God's children-
    bonafide Americans,
        citizens of the world.

One time a lonely rover, a disturbed transplant,
    now respected and redeemed,
One time an embittered 26,
    now a forgiving 62.

Enriqueta C. Mayuga

The Village of my Pain – The Valley of my Joy
(Circa 1970)

I came to this little village to make a difference,
Unfolded my soul to a needy populace –
      ignored and wanting, infirmed and needy,
I lived my Hippocratic oath -
      but insults, slander and jibes awaited me -
They did it all with impunity.
They would do anything to jeer me,
      diminish me and weaken my resolve.
But who are these people?
Where are they now?
      They - who snarled and mocked me
      with their larcenous verbiage?
      Nowhere in sight.
So what if I was misconstrued by these
      medical colleagues, self-proclaimed gurus
          ego-stricken peers past their prime,
Good deeds are incomprehensible –
      to those *incapable* of giving.

My detractors lied through their teeth,
      spouted voluminous words
          - cursing and hurling invectives.
Wasted time, wasted moments,
      misspent on jealousy and rage,
Seething their envy which knew no bounds,
Their souls empty, jaundiced and vile,
Haunted their nights - restive their days,
I could relate one to one -
      but against a pack of wolves and
sneering vipers, it was an uphill fight.
But thank goodness, those days are passé,

    Gone for good - *I hope*,

No more swipes - no more furtive glances
    or sarcastic jabs,
No more contrived rules to slice me.
It is not easy to be a trial balloon,
    a pioneer in a new land, an ethnic trailblazer
    -the only female physician
        in an all-white male enclave.
But new laws are now in place –
    on racial and gender profiling.
God gave us tenets centuries ago on greed and lust
    - inscribed on tablets and scrolls,
        not certified nor notarized,
Papers were not invented then –
Neither were congressional caucus.

My foes could not bear the idea
    that someone more capable than they
        were in their midst.
They peppered me with endless obstacles,
    stymied me at every turn,
But now God has joined the fray.
He entered the Tiananmen Square of their rampage,
He has bailed me out -
    released his projectile of righteousness.
The enlighted public, one time xenophobic,
    at last opened its eyes,
Henceforth, no more blind spots, no more racial myopia,
Gone are the pretenses and ethnic slurs – *I hope*.

Would it have been better
    if they spent their twilight years expiating
        the excrements of their failed prejudices?

Rather than baring their empty souls
    in the nursing home?
They were on top of the world, top on the tax bracket
    -the stock gurus of their time -
        basking in power politics and possessions.
Does it really matter - who really cares?
Their cronies are now gone –
    gone to Mother earth,
No more retribution by peer reviewers
    and self-proclaimed experts on trumped up charges.
My foes are now muted in their social tombs,
Their power fragmented and lost,
    denied by dementia and old age.
As one generation leaves, another arrives
    -unaware of my hurts and torments
    imposed by the unholy axis of envy,
        avarice, and prejudice.

Today, I approach my sunset
    in the spirit of forgiveness –
Time is a magic elixir with its unique condiments,
Every iota of pain and aspersion is laid to rest.
The Hippocratic oath is vibrant and well.
New forces are now at play,
    also new politics and alignments.
There are co-minglings of races and cultures,
    mixed breeds and jaded philosophies.
Marriage of contrasting pigments and
    ambiguous sex are now a fad,
Men live layered lives of multiphasic convictions -
We all search for the perfect webbing,
    vie for painless encounters.
For now – I cease to be the focus of
    envy by trabeculated souls.

Gone for good – my detractors must now face
    the wrath of a *just* and a *forgiving* God
        up there or down somewhere
I am now free from scheming foes and joyless peers
    away from spineless cohorts,
At long last –
the village of my pain
    is now the valley of my joy.

Enriqueta C. Mayuga

SECTION TWO

Smatterings of Life – Poetry

"Just when I slid out of the darkness – flew on my own wings, I began to wonder".
From: **Just When**

Just When

Just when I bade adieu
      to my vain glory days
      and pacified my yearnings –
Just when I cast aside my velvet comfort
      to plough through the beaten path,
Just when I slid out of the darkness -
      flew on my own wings –
          and glimpsed at more fulfilling prisms,
    believing that the tempest is over –
I began to wonder…

Just when I turned down the doorknobs
      to all possibilities - brood at the cards
         that I'm dealt with –
  and sulk at life's vicissitudes -
Just when I let go off the harness and discard
    the saddle,
Just when I'm about to cut my lifeline
      and give up my mooring -
Just when I thought the race is over
      and I feel depleted -
I hesitate…

Just when I grease the wheel
      to smoothen my ride -
Just when I emerge from the rubble
      of my passions –
Just when I have risen above the ashes
      and victory is within my reach,
Just when the hummingbirds are buzzing
      and the fireflies usher my luminescence,
When equity and justice is making a dent
      and humanity is winning -
I am overwhelmed –
      Just when…

Enriqueta C. Mayuga

From Both Sides Now

We give and receive –
    shut one door only to enter another,
Sometimes we borrow,
    other times we lend -
A few times we are the perpetrators
    and other times, we are the victims
        -The fall guy,
We are dented and in turn we do the denting
    "an eye for an eye" -
In many ways, in many forms –
Somehow, we have a little of Jekyl and Hyde
    in each of us.

We denounce malfeasance
    and expose run away passions,
But we ourselves have our dark and ugly side
    and can unleash graceless wrath,
O' – a lifetime of walking the tight ropes
    and teetering on the moral edge –
Skirting past missteps
    in quest of serenity.

We stifle our ears in denial
    or self-preservation,
But we cannot be dumb or be deaf in perpetuity,
We will have to face the music sometime
    as we clamber the canyons edge.

We cannot always double talk nor do double turns,
Or be able to reinvent the wheel
    nor pivot from the wrong lane,
We just *cannot nix life* because we drilled on *the wrong spot, dug the wrong hole,*
    and choose *the wrong color.*

One day chastened, our sight will be restored,
When our twilight will need more tempo
    than our choppy emotion can exude,
We can then know the difference
    between failure and success –
Between a joyless prism and a soul fulfilled.

        Enriqueta C. Mayuga

But It Hurts As Much

I may not have bruised as hard
        nor hemorrhaged as much,
I was not maimed –
        no dismantled flesh,
No twisted joints
        my mind intact
        with intellect unsullied -
Yet I hurt as much

They did not slice me
        nor uproot me – a new transplant,
            but for me, intrigue is intrigue
        slander is a slander –
And truth is not negotiable.
They could not burn my soul
        erode my ethos
            nor pillage my virtues,
But it hurts as much –
        as if they succeeded.

They could not slash my hopes
        nor blunt my dreams,
They could not still my voice
        nor efface my joy,
A vintage woman, a healer,
        with ardor to serve -
But still, I agonize as much
        with their savagery.

I feel a victim to all
        their games of inequities
Like the many preys

   who could not fight back –
   like the flower trampled –
     and the bud stunted,
I am angry that the innocent sunrise
   can be thwarted
     by disingenuous human beings.

I have not mastered
   the art of forgiving –
And I, born in pain –
   reared amidst a war
     which I cannot fathom -
cannot let go the unjustness of society
     with its selective values.

It is not easy to forgive,
   to conceal my pain
     and agonize in vain –
  when forgiving is not a word
     my foes understand,
It is not the language
   of the predators or perpetrators
     nor those with scuttled values.

I sought my God one day,
   and realized that I am not alone,
His chaste temple now permeates
   my cloistered soul –
More men have been disgraced and denied,
   bloodied and blunted –
As for me, I have learned to forgive,
But still – *it hurts as much.*

              Enriqueta C. Mayuga

We Become Who We Are

There is always a better way to clean the slate
      than starting a fight and thumping the ground.
We may see the world as black or white
      and judge human beings as good or bad.

At times we are ready to shed our joyless state
      restrain our untamed dreams –
            vanquished our tattered hopes,
A few times, we overcome our woes and wails –
      ready to spin them with wisdom learnt.
We go in and out of the revolving door
      until exhaustion fells us.

In the end, ready or not –
      accepting or not –
Whether we can discern
      the relevant from the incongruous,
      the coherent from the aberrant,
And inspite of our wants and aspirations –
      the wheels continue to grind forward, nonstop.
We must work on our mental and moral incertitude,
For mortals that we are – what we ***become***
      are not solely propelled by our genome
      nor by fate alone,
      - but from the lifestyle we have chosen.

Enriqueta C. Mayuga

Reckoning

We flip, we dive and get stranded,
If we land both feet on the ground –
      we survive and then we go on –
How cocky we can become –
      but sometimes we are chastened.
We are smitten with our own fire –
      and often ignore our fluffs and lapses,
Our passion makes us unstoppable
      and often we fail to look back.
But as the rain drops of time, catches us –
      the past becomes a blur
      and details disappear.

We are now in another world –
      a new generation has taken over,
We must hold tight to our linkage
      even the bonds are frayed
Good or bad, the wisdom learned
      becomes a deterrent to
      past mistakes,
Whatever is the messy side of our past,
      and however beautiful the memories -
We all evolve and morphe for better or for worse –
Accepting or not -
      ready or not -
We have to face our own reckoning.

Enriqueta C. Mayuga

Ain't We All?

No need to peel off my oddities,
there is no teflon left in me,
We all have stepped on egg shells,
      waded on murky waters –
          strayed on forbidden grounds.
My weak spots could also be yours.
Each of us has a blemish, a slant
      innate or acquired,
And often, we spend a lifetime
 trying to mask it.

I am not a disappearing glacier -
Unlike the clouds, which releases its mist
      and soon melt against the blazing sun,
Neither am I a flurry of snow, which thickens
      and piles up and ultimately fade -
Nor am I a worthless bleb.

I am a flood of tears at times and
      sometimes too numb to cry -
I am who I am: vulnerable, eccentric
    but oh so real -
        authentic and erratic,
Well-intentioned but oh so flawed –
Ain't we all?

Enriqueta C. Mayuga

Forgiving the Enemy

Across the boardroom is my foe:
    vile, wicked, ugly,
He is contemptuous and despicable
    a cross to bear
He treks alone – joyless,
    escapes through the revolving door
        of freedom,
How he gets away
    with his skewed ways
I do not know –
He responds to a different siren
    listens to his own sound bites,
His manners are caustic –
    his values stunted,
He is anathema to all good people
We are opposite in every sense –
    no reason to connect, to intersect
        no redeeming features –
Chiasmic our souls
    the only common thread;
We both belong to the human race
    with bare knuckles and crimson blood
        flowing through our veins,
And the only nexus is God telling us:
    We are all part of His flock
        and that somehow
            -we must try to forgive.

Enriqueta C. Mayuga

The Yang Minus The Ying
(In His Genome?)

He sneers – she fights back,

Born a fault finder –

    who only sees the joyless slug,

    the rough patches.

Always on the edge – each bruise a hemorrhage,

Haunted by every moaning leaf –

Wedded to sporadic paranoia –

-    when a lone spark from the lowly matchstick

reminds him of a fiery hell -

And vapid clouds invoke melancholia

    from the cruel storm.

He could be one's father, a lover, a foe -

A nice guy he is –

    but he nags, pushes, and presses while stressed,

He could be the celebrity, the professor, the oracle,

    the dotting father -

But he pumps his ire

    with histrionics

        spewing venom at each unwieldy score

    within his imaginary barricade.

A beaten warrior of the past –

    a jilted lover, a lost childhood, a jihadist -

Who knows?

Or maybe it is embedded in him – his genome,

Forgive him Oh Lord –

    if that is all there is to it -

But sometimes – I wonder,

    if I chose the wrong tree

        because of its alluring leaves?

If I should have chosen the sturdy roots

    buried the worthless stump

        and re-seed the famish soil -

Should I have selected the nectar instead of

favoring the wimpy petals –

    its imposing fragrance?

Did I pick a lemon, an imperfect grain

    or the town crier?

Or did I simply have a piece of the human sludge

    ----the yang minus the ying?

                Enriqueta C. Mayuga

SECTION THREE

Staples of the Soul – Essays

"We are all performers and dancers of life".
From: **Exploring the Tango of Life**

Blue Moon and Kosovo

Last night I saw the moon horizontally transected by a large blue strip more like a band dividing the full moon into two equal portions. A few minutes later, this blue band slowly dissipated; soon after a darkish hue encircled this now homogeneous moon. It was puzzling to me. I wondered what the astrologers or astronomers would say. Am I just too excited for my own naiveté? Upon reaching home, I excitedly turned on the television hoping to catch a glimpse of this phenomenon. I felt that this rarity would be splashed all over the media but I was off the mark. It was not in the 11 o'clock radio or T.V news but I felt sure it would appear in the early morning news. I prodded my husband about this occurrence and at first, he thought it was a cloud symmetrically transecting the moon but clearly it was a cloudless night. Still, I didn't elicit much enthusiasm from him. He soon agreed that this was an unusual sight and off he went to sleep. The next day, bright and early, I ran to the mailbox but neither did the morning paper, T.V or radio station mention anything about last night's occurrence. It was puzzling to me even as it further fueled my sense of curiosity.

Still wondering about the event, I related this to a friend. Apparently, what transpired was supposed to have taken place a few months ago in January. He, being Asian and Chinese, and shy by nature, he was reticent about commenting; after all, the year of the Dragon or the Tiger was not exactly making headway in my Spanish-Malayan soul. My friend, a respected intellectual who is not so inclined to soothsayers and superstitions, asked me how I view this. He looked at me waiting for more than just a perfunctory answer. I replied, "I guess it means the end of the world is coming". Then, I readily left.

Well, today is Wednesday, fifteen days from the IRS filing date; I went into full gear as I meticulously prepared my supporting tax papers. This is the day I had an appointment with my accountant and I was immersed on figuring out the details and numbers. In the process, I turned again on the T.V and still no news about the blue moon phenomena. All I could see is Kosovo with pathetic figures scurrying in the dark. This horrific scene is haunting – as I witnessed pitiful thousands of innocent people herded like cattle to the slaughterhouse. I pondered whether the absence of a God, be it Allah or Jesus, is an aftermath of this. Those who are involved in ethnic cleansing obviously are not thinking of higher ideals. It is baffling to me how men can be so cruel to each other because of ethnicity, culture and religion; how repeated torture and enslavement can transform human beings into zombies and we, the uninvolved viewers, have become callous and cynical. I changed the channel still searching for news about last night's moon phenomena but for naught. The screen continued to blare and show the melancholia of the terrorized victims as they trek through unruly and unwelcome terrain. Injuries and despair marks their lugubrious journey. Back to my journal, still half done - I am stymied and distracted in my accounting preparation. I grumble and wonder whether my figures are correct or not. As I pause, I hear the the classical music played in another channel. I thought I heard Chopin or maybe Mozart or the other way around. True, they may have different styles but composers sometimes could go off beat from their previous works. The music could also be a mellowed version of Tchaikovsky. Calmed by this immersion, I settled down. I finally finished my work in time for the accountant.

Back to the moon – I ponder its effect on me. Last night I saw the mystic sight, which elevated my imaginings. Anyone who has witnessed the luminous moon and the band that transected it this cloudless night cannot help but be stirred and touched. The experience has been transformative and ecstatic – ethereal and energizing - only to be blunted by reality of Kosovo. I turned to another channel hoping to get a glimpse again of my blue moon - or maybe a T.V reporter would somehow pick up last night's occurrence. Alas, all I could see is Kosovo – its disintegration and agony of both warring people. Not so long ago, in 1945 – Europe was devastated after a rabid dictator was obsessed in ethnic cleansing against the Jews. Almost two decades later, a lunatic ideologue in Cambodia felt it was necessary to eliminate millions of "impure" countrymen as he and his cohorts insisted on a new order. Today, the hundreds and millions of skulls on display at the Cambodian museum tells the gory barbarism of aberrant and misled human beings. Just decades ago, the same atrocities and degree of ethnic hatred happened again at the Serbia Croatian conflict. Today, ISIS, Boka Haram, El Shabab and similar hate groups continue their inhumane treatment of fellow human beings supposedly in the name of religion. It is circa 2015 and now back to my moon and the Kosovo effect on me.

Turning my eyes upward, I cried, "O' Lord, where are you?" - only to be met with stark silence. On the floor are the pages of Tolstoy and clearly written: *God sees, but lets you wait.* I guess, I can still appreciate last night's blue moon phenomena ----- *but I just have to wait – but Lord how long?*

Enriqueta C. Mayuga

Efecto (Inventory)

My mother used to call it "efecto". She would murmur to herself and sometimes loudly that she needs more efecto to keep the business going. I was barely 4 ½ years old in pre-war Philippines and her comment did not mean a thing to me. My parents owned two very popular drug stores in two adjacent towns, seven kilometers apart, one in our town of Ballesteros in the northern most province of the Philippines and nearby town of Abulog located in the same province of Cagayan. Drug stores were referred as "Farmacia". It took 30-40 minutes to commute between the two towns on gravel roads pockmarked by mud puddles. My mother was a pharmacist before she became an educator, and so was my father before he became a doctor. Years later, it finally dawned upon me that "efecto" meant inventory. In the early 1940's, it took at least 24-hours in an 800 kilometer stretch to reach Manila, the capital city of the Philippines, where all the efectos originated. The trip meant traversing a winding road on high mountain top, precipitous and narrow. It meant endless hours on unpaved roads, which turned slippery and unpassable during monsoons and rainy season – not to mention the unreliable sputtering engine. It was a big deal to have enough drugs on hand for the patients in our remote locality. The access to medicines was of important magnitude for people on the fringes and most were at poverty level. Today, I realize the foresight of my parents who were in charge of the wellbeing of so many in the most northern province of the Philippines.

I have been in private medical practice for over 44 years in Pasco, Washington as the first female obstetrician on this side of the mountain. In 1970 with barely one thousand dollars, I started my medical practice with limited inventories. It meant that the office supplies had to be ordered every week until my finances would improve. My creative receptionist scoured every second hand store in town as these were most affordable. I remember hand me down furniture, old unused clinic gowns and instruments left by doctors long before my time but were still of use. The sympathetic businessmen were open to loans as I was very much needed by the community. Ten years later, I had a new front girl who thought that my practice was busy enough that she would need to order more inventories. This time, I had the funds to pay for it. That meant ordering the usual gamut of basic office and medical supplies needed for my burgeoning medical practice at Pasco Washington. I didn't realize the specifics of what she ordered but then I was very busy. It is only now after thirty four years when I discovered that she ordered rubber bands good for another fifty years, which are now brittle and thousands of paper clips, now rusty beyond use. Of course the leftover ball pens from the original three hundred ordered have also long dried up. I do not recall what else she ordered but these events bring back memories of my mother's "farmacia" when she was always concerned about adequate inventories; she would order enough supplies to last us for six months because of the unpassable roads during the monsoon season. After 44 years in solo private medical practice, my insight on inventories has expanded. But this was not the case during my parents' time way back in the pre-war years, during Japan's occupation of the Philippines. In the United States, the roads are well paved and transportation is so accessible, so ordering by phone at a moment's notice is very simple. Well, my front girl should have applied better judgment, sometimes called common sense, when she ordered this enormous inventory. This was in the 80's. With her orders, I calculated that even at 77, I need to work another 10-15 years to finish the efectos.

I transport this experience in a broader sense at more meaningful inventories. These are the inventories of our values, good deeds, omissions and commissions. I think of inventory of good and supportive people who have been there on my ascent and some people who were not ideal inventory to have. I think of the multiple trips and ventures as I pursued my goals including the many successful attempts as well as the disappointing ones. I think of the pressures and stresses, challenges as well as obstacles, and the debacles of my journey. I am cognizant of the triumphs with the trophies, plaques, and accolades as well as the downside of my errors and judgment.

From all these experiences, I have concluded that we all should have inventories of our personal lives. My inventory should enumerate my pursuits - what I set out to do and what I actually accomplished. It also should include the accounts of good will - values retained and habits let go, virtues upheld and vices overcome.

These inventories are not unlike the paper clips and rubber bands which became brittle and useless with age. Unlike the office supplies, however, the efectos I am alluding to is life itself - the summation and totality of our human experience. Some may have maxi-dreams that did not pan out; others may have mini goals that have sprouted and enlarged. These are the events that have impacted us and have defined us, as well as the people who paved the way for us – most especially those who gave much more than we credit them for. We also have fancies of our youth that are no longer relevant to our later life. We may not recall all the specifics of past events but surely *any human being who have accomplished much could not have done so in a solitary way. In truth, we all are chained to a hierarchy of inventories of events and people.* So today, my mother still lives with me decades after she has left us. What a better way to think of efectos.

Enriqueta C. Mayuga

The Bottom Line

No matter how many places a man has been, how many people he knows and possessions he has, what counts in the end is how he relates to God and how he values his soul. In the end we must ask ourselves the inevitable question: whether our stay on earth has made someone else's life better. Like the mea culpa of the confessional, streams of questions and concerns arise from within one's soul: Was my presence a defining role to someone's existence? Did I help turn around someone's life? Have I been instrumental in lessening the evil aspirations of men? Was my support to the righteous genuine or was I too tepid to the ungodly? Am I just like any other politician – a representation of the collage in modern day America: marketable, a good communicator but detached from the concerns of the soul. Regardless of our background or inclinations, we must strive to find the reason for our being.

Our generation has become too self-indulgent and too busy with multiple pursuits. While many of these activities are positive, the efforts expounded on these distracts us from seeking a more meaningful insight of ourselves. Most concerned parents prepare their children with various disciplines to enable them to cope with the challenges and nuances ahead. Unfortunately, these involvements are the priority to the detriment of the interior life. Only a minority of the youth today find time to go inward; this actually reflects society in general. The present generation are less introspective and do not see the merit of the soul's purgation. They find religion too irrelevant, cumbersome or restrictive. The emphasis of the media on unfettered pursuit of possessions and glorifying self-experimentation further augments this attitude. Excessive emphasis on instant self-gratification and sexual aberrations defies the understanding of those born marginalized but have overcome their lot by hard work and sacrifice. They persevered and endured, they sweated and bled – like their forebears simply just to belong.

With the wave of modern scientific advances, new icons have sprouted; we have computer whiz, Star War heroes and reproductive gurus. The planetary explorations and the miracles of communication are beyond imaginings. While these achievements are laudable, these scientific and technological breakthrough have their down side. They have become mousetraps in an unintended fashion. As a result, we now have overbearing technocrats and passionate bureaucrats who rule or who have a say in every aspect of our lives. We have unimaginable comforts compared to the earlier generations - but in the process of pursuing their convenience and luxuries, we have subconsciously relegated the soul. Families have become broken and frayed and their members involved with runaway social and psychological ventures. We have too many options and are constantly gearing for upmanship – unable to separate the grain from the chaff or see the real diamond from the pebble. When the mainstream media highlights unnatural acts and aberration with nonchalance, we indeed have lost our spiritual antenna. The boundaries between carnality and bestiality are blurred. There is no more concept of sin - no concept of heaven or hell. Right and wrong is seen in the perspective of relativism.

A life well lived, is our security for inner peace and equanimity. While the believers comply with the doctrine and tenets from their religious and cultural upbringing – for nonbelievers, life simply goes on till the end of their physical existence. Inspite of our moral ambivalence or decline, all is not lost. *We have to believe that our life on this planet is just one temporary step: a prelude to the next.* Simply stated, we human beings have a soul, a God connection. ***This is incontrovertible – this is the bottom line.***

Enriqueta C. Mayuga

Those Restless Years – Never Too Late To Ruminate

We grow up as dreamers and goal seekers. Some dream more than do; others are relentless in their chosen pursuits. Still many are content to just dream – resigned as dabblers or observers of life. It is not unusual for today's youth to wind up confused in this rudderless generation, steeped with ambiguities. I had my own share of planning and sketching the life ahead of me way back in my early 20's. I continued to do this and modified my priorities as the situation called for. My focus was always success as I saw it – defined by my heroes and what my father has imbued in me. I was a fierce competitor in any involvement, be it in athletics or academics. I was always on top of my game and most of the time, I was the number one or two scorer – a valedictorian or salutatorian - but this did not come easy for me. I worked hard, studied until the wee hours in the morning and nothing got into my way of perfecting my skills and mastering the subjects, even my dreaded math classes. Science and physics humbled me but did not faze me as I studied repetitively. In the volleyball game, my killer shot intimidated my opponents and in basketball, I would never let anybody overwhelm me. Instead, I did many steals to the consternation of our opponents. I do not think that my competitors were happy with me but to me, the only thing that mattered was winning. I did my best to crush mercilessly my opponents, which was counterculture to my Filipino heritage. I always played with passion, unremitting and unstoppable. My strategy was to overcome my competitor and devastate their morale. What I lacked in innate athleticism, I made up with my ferocity – what I lacked in natural grace, I answered with tenacity and fervent determination.

As I matured, I became less of a fan of myself. In retrospect, I now realize that I was actually abrasive in the playing field. When I reflect at those graceless years, I feel a squeeze inside me. These days, I notice that I sometimes vacillate at my approach to situations and flounder at times with my decisions. There was a time when I had absolutely no qualms in my decision making and my schema for winning was winners take all. I marvel these days at how far I have bloomed and how maturity has sharpened my wit and effaced my impetuousness – how my epiphany has humbled me. As I look back, I could have improved myself if I had the sensitivity and compassion for others' feelings. I wish I treated better my opponents. I am now done holding on the ball at all cost. I simply prefer to be a spectator, an onlooker. Inside me, I still carry the specks and glitches that came with my half-baked mind, decades ago. Nowadays when I see the youth who acts like me or sometimes worse, I cringe as I recall the cocky and insecure me. I like to blame the effect on survivors like me who have experienced the cruel and oppressive Japanese invaders. I feel that my family and others like us have carried subconsciously the survivor mode that makes some of us react excessively. I believe that the tormenting years of Japanese occupation of the Philippines during World War II have left indelible marks in our psyche and have contributed to our impulsive reaction and ugliness in the playing fields of life. Some survivors have done better than others, but for many, this survival instinct – to be always be on the defensive have left a lifelong impact on our soul long after the Japanese were gone.

I am grateful to have the chance to refine and rectify my philosophical stance. My account is not unique – it is the story of every human being who has lived on the fringes and has been in the throes of death. It is the story of overcoming obstacles with intensity, sometimes with ferocity. It is a survivor story. I carried this attitude of competiveness even when I came to America in 1963 at the heart of civil rights strife. The youth in me impaled by idealism was bent on winning. The attitude carried me through – when I entered private practice as the first female ethnic specialist in Eastern Washington and the Tri-Cities was basically an all-white enclave.

These days, I mull over my epiphany and reflect back at those graceless years in a kinder stance. I believe I have gone as far as I can in this secular setting. I am somewhat ambivalent of "success" as interpreted by less altruistic human beings. *With age, comes wisdom and humility - with epiphany, comes refinement and sophistry.* Above all, there is *indescribable serenity* and *poetry* from within that is almost surreal.

Enriqueta C. Mayuga

Soul In Ice

I have a confession to make - a frightening revelation. I believe I have lost my fire even perhaps my soul. The other day my niece mentioned to me about the mass murders in Romania. All I found myself asking was, "What weapons were used for these grisly acts? Did they use gas? Poison? Knives? Again last week, the newspapers trumpeted the news that the Azerbaijanis were being shot by the Soviets, witnessed by the neighboring Armenians who applauded it. I was curious about the specifics of the celebration by the Armenians. Somehow I became more engrossed with the details of their festive response rather than be shocked by the atrocities. Another headline from the tabloid, The Enquirer, was about a 60-year-old grandmother from South America who volunteered her womb to carry on a transplanted embryo for the sake of her barren daughter. I probed the legitimacy and legality of the offspring and conjectured on the constitutionality of this situation. I was also immersed on the question whether the sperm donor had undergone AIDS testing. I wondered whether the medical insurance extended to both parties. So distracted was I with these concerns that I failed to question the moral aspect of this transaction.

Inundated with scandals and men's dalliances, today the word "sin" no longer applies. Acid and genetic experimentation is the norm. All what the lawyers and the legislators require is legal transparency, regardless of the transgression; group sex and drug uses are common day happenings. Our country spends massive amounts of resources on sexual aberrations, drug addictions and criminal wrongdoings. In my opinion, they are not very effective because the direction is more for probity of the psyche and the intellect with convoluted assumptions and no clear cut conclusions. On the other end of the spectrum is the punitive all or none stance by hardliners of government policies. They leave the transgressors with no hope of being rehabilitated.

Subconsciously, the "shock" effect from this occurrence has insidiously left me. I find myself inured to the ongoing misdeeds and perversions. My mind is numb with the monstrosity of men's invasion and his capacity for misadventures – and the unapologetic propensity for crossing the line. Like a leper, the sensitivity of my fingertips is lost. In another time I would have prayed for the victims of these mass murders even as I would pray also for the perpetrators; time was that I would have led a crusade against men's tampering of the embryo and the invasion of the natural biological process. I called Test-tube babies a clear case of microscopic adultery. I have previously deemed surrogate motherhood and fatherhood as the devil's concoction but now I am no longer appalled by these revelations. Heinous acts no longer malign my sense of righteousness; I have become accustomed to blasphemies and slowly transformed into a cynic and a skeptic.

I used to oppose with all my might and power the atrocities committed by men against his fellow human being. Incest was incest, stealing was stealing and killing was plain destruction of human life; prostitution was evil. Now incest though not legal is tolerated by some liberals as a way of life of certain sects. These social thinkers surmise that certain accommodations could be entertained, in spite of the deceit and deception of these perpetrators on their young and vulnerable victims. Insider information regarding stocks becomes illegal only when one is exposed and caught. Stealing is merely deemed as a transfer of ownership or misappropriation and only punishable if not sanctioned by law. Pro-choice proponents argue that freedom to select the options for unwanted pregnancy is paramount even though the unborn child, a gift of God, should be protected like any adult human being. To many, prostitution and voyeurism, though unsavory habits should be tolerated. This *culture of acquiescence* is pervasive in this present generation which *caters to a life of frills and frothy comfort.*

I came to America, a good Filipino bent on selling the best of the Philippines and incorporating the good in America. I intended to go back to that exquisite land to fight the onslaught of ignorance and corruption. Now I find myself sitting back in my rocking chair pondering the things that might have been. Momentarily, I realized that I am sipping English tea, which taste like a mix of cinnamon and mint or maybe it could also be a mix of tangy orange and mint. Somewhat guilty at this self-indulgence, I long for moral clarity. I feel powerless about all the misdeeds and malfeasance before me and *how little I can effect a change.*

My fellow human beings – do not judge me harshly because of this sense of detachment and helplessness. Wait till the last flaming tinder within me is squelched. Condemn me not, simply because I have lost my fire; sadly, ***my soul is in ice.***

Enriqueta C. Mayuga

Staying With The Fundamentals

People are always moving and leaving, bidding welcome and bidding goodbye. Time after time we keep looking for our niche, where we fit and where we could finally find acceptance in our terms. In this process we forgive, we promise and we even renege. Some of us are more intense than others. The discovery of a new DNA molecule might excite the geneticist but to many, this event might evoke simply a cursory interest. Some of us dream more than others but many are better storytellers. One time we are the winners, in another time - losers. We constantly live in a whirlpool of events, enviable and dynamic but often times beyond our imaginings and control. In some instances we are undermined and in another – we undermine others. Life is a tee and a tat. We need to be sensitive and sensible, open and well grounded.

In our youth, we are consumed with passion, be it romantic or ideological. We see nothing in the horizon to deter us from our visions. We fiercely react to those who disparage our race, our creed and become very defensive. We are filled with ire as we witness injustices on the defenseless. When we reach adulthood, we are more tempered and any signs of the rebel in us have dissipated. We learn to co-exist and appreciate the art of working together in a system that is not always friendly and kind. Our objectives may still be the same, but the approach to the problem is done with civility. As we enlarge our prism, we are more effective and less embroiled in controversies and recriminations. No longer do we have the knee-jerk reactions to those who wronged us or those who have wantonly disregarded our rights and even slandered us. Instead, we regroup and recoup. Aware of our limited resources and impending mortality, we opt for meaningful priorities. Better to lose some battles in order to gain more in the end; better to suffer minor bruises than from searing wounds, which takes lifetime to heal.

Life is like a boxing bout with different judges monitoring every round. If the twelfth round is reached with no knockdowns, the winning points will be awarded to the winner. At my age, I now go for the winning, not necessarily the knockouts. There is no such thing as permanent victory, permanent defeat, or perpetual joy. We can make our triumphs last beyond our present victory when we do not pummel the losers to perpetual ignominy. *From defeat we become innovative, creating situations and opportunities that propel us to higher planes.*

With the march of time, the impact of age on our fledgling body becomes obvious. We also become more conciliatory and worry about personal needs, which in the past we were dismissive off. We are now focused on better hearing aids, reading glasses and comfortable foot wears. We want medication that we can easily swallow and pills to improve our memory. We petition for better laws to insure stability of Medicare and social security. We lobby our congressman for protection of the salmon, the spotted owls and friendly bees. We insist that the river path should be more senior friendly and not be used as a lover's lane for youthful dalliances. We are cognizant of our health needs and the disruptions caused by economic and political upheavals. We denounce runaway malpractice suits and disdain legal skirmishes. We look at the widespread abuse of drugs, family breakdown and racism as symptomatic of our failed generation. More than ever, we have come to realize that *human solutions alone are not adequate to stave off these misfortunes.* We realize that some conflicts could be fully resolved – but a few never.

Life is like a graduation of sort. It may take time to get a degree or a diploma, much deserving as we are. A final commencement will take place in time, but again it may be postponed or deferred. Situation differs. There is a higher plane of justice with varying paradigms, which looks at life in toto, not unlike the boxing bout described earlier. We must stay focused on the right trajectory: family, fellowship, unswerving faith and trust in our Maker. *Simply stated, we need to stick with the fundamentals.*

Enriqueta C. Mayuga

Living On The Fringes

With my looming age of 77, I refuse to return to my habits of internalizing the bygone times. I will no longer rationalize why things turn out the way they do or why bad things happen to good people. No one person can resolve problems that are innate to human existence. Instead, I will redirect my energy to what is doable. I am past ruminating over my childhood of possibilities. My textured life no longer bothers me. Life is too complicated and intricate to ferret out its wart and pockmarks. It would be just an exercise of futility. I will not incessantly pursue philosophical concepts especially if they are speculative or mindboggling. If the Freudian theory is alluring, if not titillating during its time – so be it. If Karl Marx's, "Das Kapital", has attracted many restless segment of social thinkers a generation ago, let it rest on its own merit. After all, his philosophy had been debunked – communism has turned out to be a failure. My curiosities may be far reaching but they should not be implacable nor should they interfere in positive and productive endeavors. I realize that my focus should not be all about me but what will come next. I must look at the bigger picture and where I stand in my adopted country of five decades.

The potholes of politics as evident in the last presidential election deters me from contemplating the best but I must move on, regardless of my gut feeling and my visceral response to the hypocrisy of our politicos. I may have been lured by the promises of well-meaning candidates but I am also realistic to what is possible and pragmatic for our country.

When I came to America in 1963 – at the age of 26, I exuded untold joy and delight being in a country, which Filipinos equated to a Utopia. This was in mark contrast over six decades prior when America was the enemy, treacherously colonizing the Philippines. The Filipinos have barely overthrown the oppressive Spanish regime of over 350 years when the United States took over militarily and politically (in the treaty of Paris). This was in the late 1899. America soon rebounded, opening mass education to the people promoting women suffrage and civil rights even exceeding the progress in mainland America. This endeared them to the people. The American concepts of freedom and equal justice have come to a fruition: the great experiment was succeeding.

I know now that the streets of America are not paved with gold but I am proud to be a part of its compelling call where individual freedom is highly prized and justice is touted as a right of each citizen. Sadly, in my opinion, this is not exactly taking place today. It is also unfortunate that our nation is polarized. Being rewarded for one's effort is not a notion that is original in this country, but centuries of the grand experiment have shown that the American Dream of being rewarded for one's effort is still true for those who are willing and able.

With five decades here, I am a witness to the ups and downs of the economic trails and the socio-politico fiasco, which our nation is now embroiled. I am also saddened by the regression of values and degradation of mores. The progress in civil rights and the many scientific breakthroughs are exemplary but are beclouded by the moral downside. Everything is a mixed bag. I still like to subscribe to the philosophy that decency and worthiness should be extolled.

America, the one I knew in 1963, has evolved and is no longer a lily white country, but the basics of its founders and pioneers should be upheld. Today, this nation's textures and trajectories have changed. There is wobbliness of ethics and character. Some of our politicos have envisioned that they could engineer virtues - and have therefore allowed trendy inclinations of people with marginal characters to lead us. America is no longer a white country – the one I found when I migrated here in June 1963. Frankly it does not bother me. After all, in the eyes of our creator, ethnicity and race does not count. I am not sure, however, how long we can continue exulting galleries of leaders with barren and dotted backgrounds and surly outlooks. It is beyond me to even think I can be a factor in salvaging lost values and stripped virtues. We may not be able to replicate the heroism of our founders nor the heroics of good men all over the world but certainly by living good lives and adhering to moral and spiritual tenets – we may be able to stymie the decline. In spite of this, we must not give up. We need to hold our ground and trust that better times are ahead. We, human beings, belong to a higher and more noble governance – beyond the potholes of lesser men and unworthy leaders. Our faith emphasizes and history teaches us that the good will eventually prevail.

At 77, with years fully lived, I feel that we are teetering on the margins of an ambivalent times; *simply we are living in the fringes.*

Enriqueta C. Mayuga

Staying The Course

How would you like to do away with the pretenses and shenanigans of failed relationships and instead go back to the basics. As a young bride or groom especially in the nascency of romance, the enigma and mystics of marriage or togetherness is exciting and exhilarating. Curiosity and enthusiasm is encompassing. How time can alter our perspectives when we reach 40 or even 80. With the mechanics of daily existence wrought with boredom and drudgery, and sometimes with harshness and hopelessness, we often feel trapped with repetitive irrelevance. As we age, we often tend to view lightly our success. At times we are dismissive of the stability, peace, and satisfaction derived from it. A few of us are constantly searching – and never seem satisfied.

When we are young, we dream and aspire; this aspiration spurs us to pursue zealously our goals. We grapple with barriers – endure and persevere, ready to bleed in this pursuit. We rummage through our wealth of energy with zest and passion. At some point having achieved our objectives, we start questioning the coherence of our lives – some do more than others – triggered by a society that has redefined success and substituted altruism with a culture of materialism. Felled by financial and health debacles, or political and career upheavals, we become pensive and contemplative. We see a generation strutting their material acquisitions with flair. Emotionally dislodged, we are attracted to the cajolers of fleeting joys and the carolers of aberrant lifestyles whose flagship is social experimentation. In the process, we take for granted our accomplishments and even forget the sufferings and sacrifices that festooned it. We start to wonder if we have missed out on the good life or took the wrong train.

The human story is not a perfect story. In this digital and computerized world with continuous demands for instant result and unending consumption, we often get waylaid. We should not forget that life is in a constant flux, dynamic and evolving. Though we may not always remain the poster child of enduring success, we should not feel left behind or believe that we lost out. We must not nullify our past struggles just because we are derailed by exhaustion and old age or that things did not go our way. We can be malleable without being pulled down to the gutters. A new generation, unaware of our vicissitudes should not transform us into skeptics and cynics – just because a band of avant-gardes have taken the center stage. There's no need to redefine success and uproot our sense of rectitude and decency simply because we are on some career and economic low. Maybe we are destabilized by dissonant relationships – a marriage that did not pan out or a friendship that has gone sour but we must keep the faith. We must remain unflappable even as we can be pliable. It is very helpful to roll back the video of our past and take pride in our triumphs and accomplishments. One day we will overcome our woes and regain back our stability- back to our elements of comfort and sense of dignity.

Each decade has its own faddish imprint. Today it is Twitter and Facebook; tomorrow will bear its own. We must stay alert and sensitive to the subtleties of human interaction and never take it for granted. We must not allow our identities to be smudged nor our values to be subverted. Let trifles be trifles. Let aberrant style withstand the test of time; it is convoluted enough without always confronting it. Let no one impinge or uproot our sense of innocence. No amount of crisis justifies ignoring the fundamentals. We all have our beginnings but we can also morph for the better. Having gone through this journey of purpose, we must stay the course – same lane, same zeal, same fervor.

Exploring The Tango Of Life

Sooner or later, we, all, will experience the tango of life – some more than others. The adept glides and sways gracefully – reminiscent of the ballerina in the Black Swan classic. Others are even more dramatic, not unlike the soprano belting her aria before thousands of adoring and mesmerized fans. With valentino-like aura, hair combed tightly on the sides – chin up, the heroe takes long strides and with faraway gaze, he leads his partner in one direction. Suddenly, he reverses his steps, goes back to the opposite direction. With a dominant motion – he lets her go swirling, until both meet each other in tandem as they resume the promenade of life. At times, she huffs and puffs – determined to meet her partners clasp in the enduring mystic of the dance.

Some dancers merely go with the flow, performing careful steps and turns – satisfied to be reunited with their partner. Others are able to step up in unison with the melody through the sensuously demanding and emotional trying process; still others keep trying – sweating it out in bits and pieces – these difficult to execute steps. They merit admiration for their persistence even if they are less genetically endowed. What they lack in grace, they compensate with their perseverance – eventually they learn the steps, make the grade, becoming the best teachers and role model of their peers. Humbly they accept their peripheral role realizing that not all can be the leading dancers. There is only one main soprano, only one winning tenor, only one lead dancer. But what truly matters in any performance, tango or otherwise, is the heart and resilience of the performers – the ability to adjust and adapt. Some of us are better doing the waltz or cha-cha; others prefer the boogie, rhumba or lombada – not unlike athletes who are better in one game than the other. This is analogous to the painters who have various preferences for different medium.

Whatever we set out to do or accomplish, we must understand the beginning act, the transition and the finale. We need to go with the beat and rhythm – even if one partner missteps and especially when the music misplays. We can always outperform one another on the dance floor of life's arena as skillful artists and survivors do, but at what price? *Excellence is admirable but fervency and discipline supersedes it all.*

What happens when the dance is over? Can we claim that we have exceeded expectations? What happens when we are at the pinnacle of our performance? Should we be content with our laurels? In life, each of us will experience a moment of triumph whether we are exemplary individuals or simply a part of life's mosaic. In the tango – the steps are so dramatic. After gracefully whirling and undulating to the music – who would not revere the moment when we finally reunite with our partner. Life is like a tango and almost always, we find a partner but not all partnerships last and bonding could be complex. Those with the innate gift of grace and resilience could often find a way to make it work.

Indeed, we are all performers and dancers of life; the tango exemplifies the *discipline, the precision and also the thrill.* We go through the ebb and flow, the recurring twists and turns with variation of the theme. We may have the swagger and the glide but those alone do not suffice.

We need synchrony and coherence so that the melody coalesce with the mood. We must continue the quest for excellence, partner or no partner as this is the pragmatic approach to the real dance of life.

It is not alone the dancer or the singer but the song; *the music with the tempo and the zest when put together is the winning number* – the one that counts in the *real* tango of life.

Enriqueta C. Mayuga

SECTION FOUR

The Lighter Side of Life

"Let me release my own arrow, track my own trail – and I will be what you want me to be – the manchild of your parental yearnings".

From: **The Manchild of Your Yearnings**

Big Sem - My Kind Of Dude

There he is - strutting with his fancy boots
      silver spurs shining against the blazing sun,
His faded jacket parched by the elements
      speaks of the journey he endured.
The swagger is still there -
      stride stymied by age and time,
His dark lens mask his droopy lids,
Leather hat pummeled by countless brawls
      at faraway taverns where
      desperate men lost their cool.
He hides his wobbly arms
      finger ready to cock the trigger and blast the foe -
He gazes ahead like Clint Eastwood in "Dirty Harry"
      or like Gary Cooper of "High Noon Fame",
 He is not there to face a traitor or avenge his honor -
      at least not at this age,
Past a weather beaten life – through with his old style -
This fabled man dubbed as Big Sem
      is no longer a threat -
Simply checking his car at the public lot
      less a vandal jumped on it in the dark of night,
But do not be deceive – I will vouch for him
      He is still a force to contend with -
This hunk of a man – a kind man
      may be past his heyday -
But he is my *kind* of a dude.

Enriqueta C. Mayuga

I Did It My Way

I didn't get in
    I just didn't fit – ethnic, foreign, woman,
I didn't play my cards well,
    my dreams scooped
        from my very eyes,
I didn't play their game,
    didn't join the club-
    I would be rejected anyway,
I put on a mask
    refused the role assigned to me,
The missing piece in the slate
    was not for me –
    who dared big dreams.

My spirit free-
    refused to abide to their
        laws of absurdities:
    their portable virtues-
    their contempt of the culture,
        shrouded with pettiness and hypocrisy.

When I will go on-
    someday soon,
I will be content
    that I lived my creed,
    and fought with ardor
Like a spirited woman
    suffering from the brunt of my convictions
That I stuck to my guns
    and did it my way
        …even if I didn't get in.

Enriqueta C. Mayuga

Am Ready For The Bloom

At the sound of spring

and its cherished vibes,

The root awakens

from its ritual sleep,

The skeletal twig

parades it embryonic bud-

Soon to unfurl

its long-awaited bloom,

Ready to retake the world

with its spiraling joy,

Once more, I await a new beginning

another chance to play-

revel in my own repertoire-

perhaps my last?

Enriqueta C. Mayuga

And People Think I Am Normal

I never made the grade,
    never the insider,
I followed the script to a T
    beholden to the secular pied piper.
I shed of my comely *kimono* –
Let go of my warbled accent –
No more of the barrio lass in me –
    my linkage to the past effaced.

Gone are the *kundiman* of my youth
    - the tango of my father's vintage,
Grand Meniere and Don Perignon,
    vodka and pot are in.
I revered the spotlight those times,
    awashed with tinsel town drama,
Wall Street was my crowd –
Ferrari and Lamborghini, my altar.

But all things do come to an end –
    I am a living witness to my scars,
Coming to America is both a boon and a curse,
A nebulous 40 years – a drifter in a hedonistic drama,
I am back where I started –
    prior to my pugilistic ways
But now an enlightened 77.
Vanities of all vanities,
    -am back at the starting line
    indented and remorseful,
        irrelevant to the youth –
But very much in control.
Insider or outsider be it so –
    it doesn't really matter now –
Coherent and contrite – I am at peace
    -also known as *clown philosopher,*
People think that I had it good –
    they think I am normal
    whatever normal is.

Enriqueta C. Mayuga

When I'm Gone

When I go, weep not –
        no shrill voice, no sobs, no wails,
Be of sound countenance –
        no excess verbiage or tasteless jokes,
Do not feign sadness
        avoid flimsy utterances
Enough that this word is teeming
        with societal pretenses,
When asked about me – do not hedge,
Speak not of my tears, my fears, nor my losses,
        only my good deeds – not my misdeeds,
Talk as if I am still around, in your presence –
Temper your voice – do not scream but neither be boring,
I dislike lack of candor but much more than that –
        I abhor anyone who talks with no vocal inflection.
If unable to highlight my attributes in two minutes –
        then be quiet,
Each person can be described in a few lines or two sentences,
        I do not subscribe to platitudes – especially to monotones,
When my coffin will be laid to rest –
        avoid jerky remonstrances –
No flailing of the arms, no beating of the chest, no panting –
Do not cry behind your chador –
Save the copious tears to moisten the cactus or the orchids –
Even in grief, we need to go green.

Be genuine, be concise –
Brevity should be your style –
        no anecdotes, no disjointed verses, no tall tales,
You can quote me
        but leave other authors lone,
Do not open my dark side or expose my missteps,

Leave my imperfections alone –
Cast aside my ineptitudes,

Ignore the tsunami of my passions,
Mince no unkind words –
I never claimed to be lily-pure,
      but neither was I a vixen.
Do not reveal my age, my weight, my unpaid bills,
      the placement of my tattoos, my tongue ring,
           especially my dalliances with
           underserving men of token background,
Speak no more of my unrequited love,
      the lovers I spurned or who jilted me.
Do not mention the accolades I did not deserve-
      nor the trophies and my medals which deluded me,
Forget that I exiled my in-laws to a distant land,
Just recall that I became a rabble-rouser for good causes,
      and in my later years made up for the skirmishes with my foes,
Just impress that I did these all in style,
      and have given much of myself for redemption,
Do not mention the likes of Lady Gaga or Tiny Tim-
      though I can put up with Elton John or Ricky Martin.

I bid adieu – so be at peace,
      as I march to a *forgiving* land
Where my secrets are safe
      and no one would give a hoot about my skeletons,
And *only* the crosses I carried to reach my God
Are all that truly matter.

                                              Enriqueta C. Mayuga

The Manchild of Your Yearnings

Let me release my own arrow,

trek my own trail

glide my own plane-

I may fall and crash

to oblivion where I will be consigned,

But if I can avoid the fall

-reverse my downslide,

I will come out a better human being

who will carry his own spear,

sing his own aria,

grind his own stone

And I will be what you want me to be

-the man-child of your parental yearnings.

Enriqueta C. Mayuga

Romance Comes Late To My Life

Just when I am about to
        hang my clothes for the winter –
        store the frills that
             embellish my body,
Just when I have found my own moorage
        and clipped my wings –
        onward to the dormant meadows –
Just when I am at the end of the long pasture
        calling it quits for the forbidden games
        that used to amuse me,
My ventures wild –
        Climbing Matsu Pecho, the Himalayas
        Sailing on the turbulent Pacific
Just when ----
        I found *r*omance

Tis' not the romance that you think –
        no errant party has entered my heart,
After all, I am married for 50 years
        my callous hands to show and
        many twinkling stars which
            saturated my dreams have vanished.
Children now grown ups
        -parents now gone,
And the calming waves that comes when
        the battle is done.
It is simply that I have found a new romance –
        sizzling under each spell
        of budding truth and serene thoughts
I am in love with life!

Enriqueta C. Mayuga

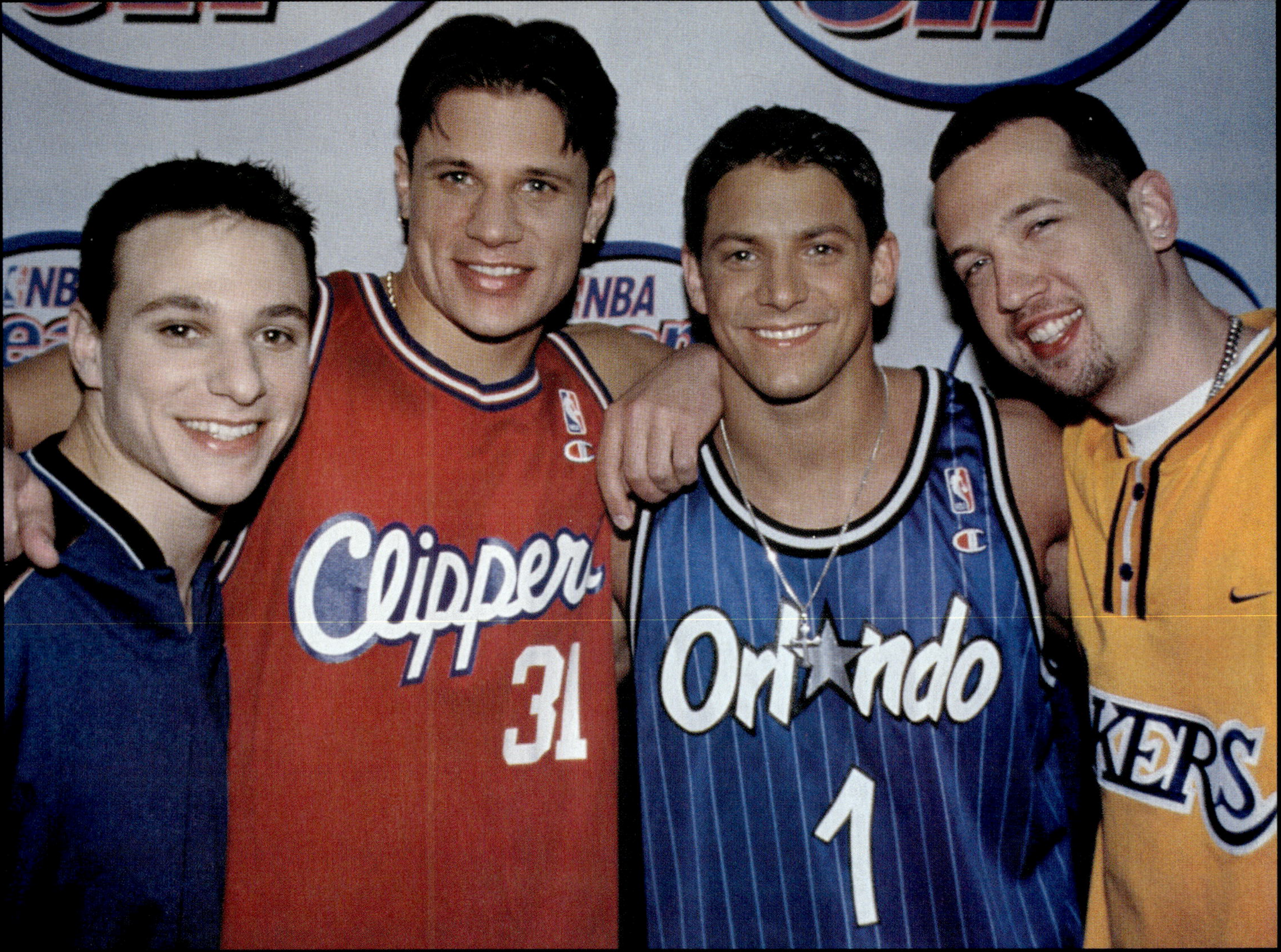
NBA
NBA
31
Orlando
1
KERS

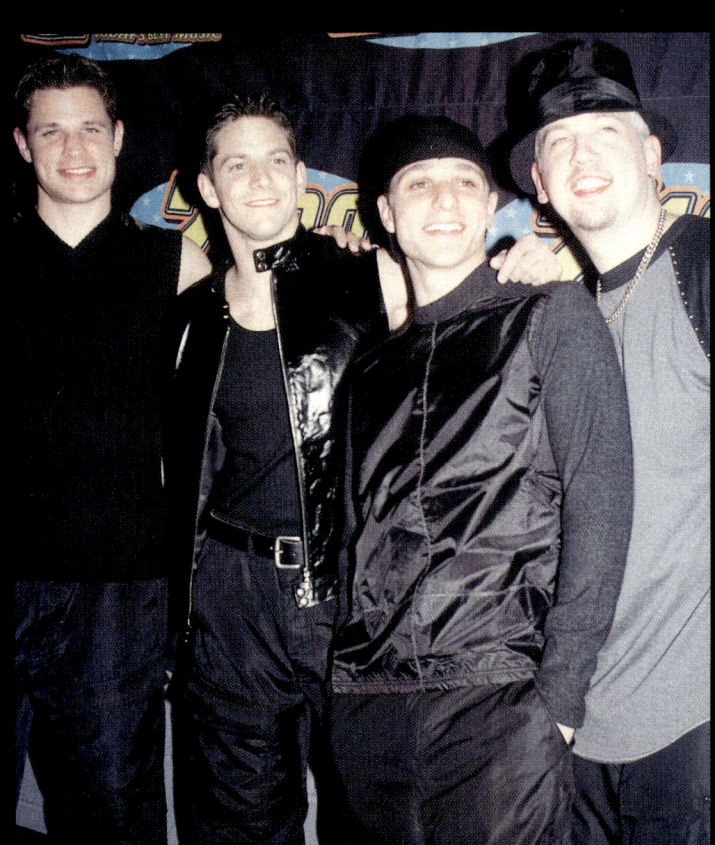

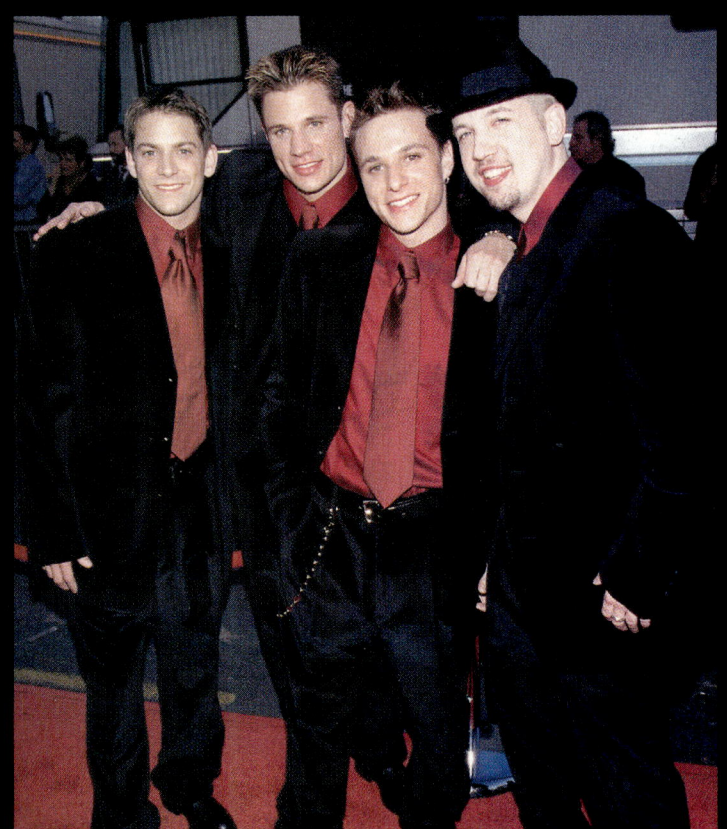

Caught On Film

THIS PAGE, CLOCKWISE FROM UPPER LEFT: LISA ROSE/GLOBE PHOTOS; TOM RODRIGUEZ/GLOBE PHOTOS; MARY MONACO/SHOOTING STAR; MELANIE EDWARDS/RETNA LTD.; KATHY HUTCHINS/HUTCHINS PHOTO AGENCY; FITZROY BARRETT/GLOBE PHOTOS; JILL JOHNSON/HUTCHINS PHOTO AGENCY; STEVE GRANITZ/RETNA LTD. OPPOSITE PAGE, CLOCKWISE FROM TOP: ERNIE PANICCIOLI/RETNA LTD.; FITZROY BARRETT/GLOBE PHOTOS; FRANK WHITE

film

ANSWERS

1. a	21. a
2. a	22. b
3. b	23. a
4. b	24. b
5. a	25. a
6. a	26. a
7. c	27. d
8. d	28. c
9. b	29. d
10. b	30. a
11. b	31. b
12. c	32. b
13. a	33. c
14. d	34. b
15. c	35. a
16. b	36. c
17. c	37. b
18. a	38. c
19. c	39. a
20. c	40. d

HOW DID YOU DO?

35-40 CORRECT
YOU MUST BE NUTS OVER 98°!

Not everyone gets a score like this. My goodness! We couldn't fool you with any of our trick questions. Are you sure you're not related to one of the guys? Or personal friends with Nick, Jeff, Drew and Justin? We just hope something good comes out of this obsession of yours. (Have you thought about writing to MTV's Fanatic? Or being president of their fan club?) And if you haven't started a 98° Web site, we suggest you get moving on that. Go on, what are you waiting for?

27-34 CORRECT
YOU'RE A SIZZLIN' HOT FAN

Whenever 98° is in your town, we know where you are – standing in line waiting to see them up close and personal. And we also know who's on the phone every day voting for their videos, making sure they'll be on TRL. 98° is very lucky to have a devoted fan like you. You're the reason why they're so popular. (You should feel so proud.) But by the looks of your score, we can also tell there's room in your CD player for other groups, like Backstreet Boys and LFO. (Even though 98° gets the most play!)

20-26 CORRECT
LUKEWARM LISTENER

You groove to their tunes, and like to read articles written about them, but your love for 98° pretty much stops there, right? You're not an obsessed fan. (You may not even know their last names.) But you certainly don't change the dial when "I Do" comes blaring through your stereo. In fact, you're probably a big fan of other R&B groups like Jodeci and Boyz II Men. If you're diggin' 98° more and more every day and want to know all the juicy details about the boys, read the rest of this magazine and check out their official Web site, www.98degrees.com.

LESS THAN 20 CORRECT
DON'T KNOW MUCH ABOUT 98°, HUH?

Hmmm. You probably didn't buy this mag, did you? In fact, you may have borrowed it from your friend who is a big fan. But you must like their music (it's hard not to), because you wouldn't have picked it up to begin with. Well, we suggest you keep reading this Gold Collectors Series issue. We not only guarantee you'll end up being a fan of 98° – they're the nicest, sweetest, cutest, most talented foursome around – but we know that if you come back and take this quiz again, you'll up your score to the "sizzlin' hot fan" category.

Test Your 98° I.Q.

29. The name 98° is perfect. It matches the guys' personalities, looks and music, of course. But they almost chose several other names, including:
a) Quads and Smooth Ones
b) Foursome and Cool Guys
c) 3 Plus 1 and Harmony
d) Just Us and Verse Four

30. But they finally picked 98° because:
a) it represents the heat and passion of their music.
b) Nick was taking his temperature the day they were thinking of names.
c) Jeff's mom liked that name.
d) they couldn't agree on any other name.

31. Diane Warren is amazing. She's written tons of songs. So you can imagine how thrilled 98° was when they got to record one of her ballads. What's the name of this awesome tune?
a) "Tell Me Now"
b) "Was It Something I Didn't Say"
c) "Can You Read My Lips"
d) "You're Hurtin' My Heart"

32. 98° are totally talented. In fact, they'll probably be around for many years to come, which is why this female superstar asked them to perform on her album. Do you know who she is?
a) Madonna
b) Mariah Carey
c) Celine Dion
d) Janet Jackson

33. Which of these models played the lead girl in the one of their most popular videos, "I Do"?
a) Daisy Fuentes
b) Cindy Crawford
c) Ali Landry
d) Halle Berry

34. Whew! Are you tired yet? Well, you've got a few more to go. So answer this: What's Justin's biggest pet peeve?
a) when people don't look him in the eye
b) when people smoke cigarettes
c) when people call him Justy
d) when people litter

35. Drew's got his pet peeve, too. Do you have any clue what it is? Any idea? Put it this way: Just make sure you get a manicure before you ever hang out with him. He hates:
a) dirty fingernails
b) dirty ears
c) smelly perfume
d) smelly armpits

36. Justin said if he weren't in 98°, he'd be a:
a) snorkeling instructor
b) fireman
c) history teacher
d) piano player

37. Breakfast is Jeff's favorite meal of the day, and one thing he loves to eat is:
a) bagels
b) omelets
c) bacon
d) grits

38. They're naturals on stage, but Justin, Jeff, Nick and Drew aren't so comfortable with doing what?
a) taking photos
b) being interviewed
c) dancing
d) singing on stage

39. Who loves to take pictures of every place they visit while touring around the world?
a) Drew
b) Nick
c) Justin
d) Jeff

40. Well, you've made it. Exhausted? Don't worry, we'll make this one an easy question: The boys are back with a new CD (Yay!). We're sure it's going to be just as awesome, if not better, than their other ones. What's the name of it, anyway?
a) "Running On Empty"
b) "We're Back, and Hotter Than Before"
c) "99°"
d) "Revelation"

Now see how you did!

16. Speaking of Jeff, he's pretty picky when it comes to girls. He hasn't found his soulmate yet, but when he does, she'll definitely have these qualities:
a) nice eyes and great hair
b) an awesome personality and nice eyes
c) a great laugh and perfect teeth
d) skinny arms and perfect teeth

17. Quick: What's Drew's trademark?
a) his smile
b) his laugh
c) his baseball cap
d) his special way of dancing

18. Besides singing with the boys and flying all over the world to spend time with his sweetie, Jessica Simpson, Nick likes to:
a) watch sports
b) camp
c) fish
d) eat hotdogs

19. Slowly but surely, the four guys got together to form the group. But it took a lot of convincing for this cutie to take the risk. Which guy was the last one to join?
a) Jeff
b) Nick
c) Drew
d) Justin

20. But there's a reason why it took a lot of convincing for the answer to number 19 to join. He was really enjoying his job, which was:
a) working as a photographer at a newspaper
b) selling life insurance over the phone
c) working as an emergency medical technician
d) training to become a physical trainer

21. You may have gotten the last two questions right, which means you know who was the last to JOIN the group. But do you know which of the four hotties actually STARTED the group? (We're sure the other three are thanking him now!)
a) Jeff
b) Nick
c) Drew
d) Justin

22. Although they're on the Universal Records label now, which company discovered 98° and first signed them?
a) Geffen
b) Motown
c) Interscope
d) Atlantic

23. Jeff's got more charisma in his pinky than most guys have in their whole body. So it's no surprise that he was in the acting field before the group got together. In fact, he was in a commercial for:
a) Coke
b) Pepsi
c) The Navy
d) Burger King

24. While we're on the topic of Jeff, answer this question: What was he studying while attending Kent State University?
a) English
b) psychology
c) engineering
d) theater

25. Everyone who's anyone knows by now that Nick and Drew are brothers. But they're not the only children in the Lachey family. How many siblings do they have?
a) 4
b) 3
c) 2
d) 1

26. Justin's role in the group is key. Without him, well, they'd be missing an important sound. While Nick and Jeff are tenors, Justin is the:
a) bass
b) tenor
c) soprano
d) treble

27. Which two guys performed together throughout high school?
a) Justin and Jeff
b) Jeff and Nick
c) Nick and Drew
d) Justin and Nick

28. Is there a special lady that warms Justin's heart? Maybe. But there's definitely an actress that he considers his fave. (Too bad she's taken!)
a) Goldie Hawn
b) Ashley Judd
c) Reese Witherspoon
d) Sarah Michelle Gellar

Test Your 98° I.Q.

4. 1999 was a big (and successful) year for 98°, but when did the fine foursome first start singing together?
1. 1997
2. 1995
3. 1996
4. 1998

5. Hey, everyone's gotta start somewhere, right? Well, during what event did 98° sing the National Anthem?
a) Los Angeles Dodgers baseball game
b) New York Giants football game
c) New York Yankees baseball game
d) 1999 Super Bowl

6. We know that Jeff, Drew, Nick and Justin inspire us in many ways, but which group has inspired them and their music?
a) Take 6
b) Crosby, Stills, Nash and Young
c) The Jackson 5
d) Soundgarden

7. Which of these pop princesses opened up for 98°? (Hint: She often gives her own "sweet kisses" to one of the guys in the group.)
1. Mandy Moore
2. Britney Spears
3. Jessica Simpson
4. Hoku

8. There's nothing like home sweet home. That's why brothers Nick and Drew love to visit their hometown, which is:
a) Toledo, Ohio
b) Memphis, Tennessee
c) Albany, New York
d) Cincinnati, Ohio

9. Before he joined the group, this singing sweetie spent his time being studious. Where did Nick go to college?
a) University of Miami, Florida
b) Miami University of Ohio
c) New York University
d) Notre Dame University

10. Growing up, Nick said he always dreamed about playing this sport professionally.
a) baseball
b) football
c) hockey
d) tennis

11. While his brother Nick was in college, Drew was off spending his time doing something else. He wasn't in school, he was:
a) flipping burgers at McDonald's
b) in the Army
c) traveling around Europe
d) training to become a beautician

12. He can sing, he can sorta dance and he has a face that lights up the room. And don't get us started on his bod. He's buffer than buff, which is why the guys in the group call Nick:
a) Rocky
b) Mr. T
c) Quadzilla
d) He Man

13. Like Christina Aguilera, 98° recorded a song for Disney's "Mulan" soundtrack. This may be a tricky one, but if you're their No. 1 fan you'll know that the name of the song is:
a) "True To Your Heart"
b) "You're The One"
c) "You Gotta Be You"
d) "Hey Now, Girl. Be Mine"

14. There's another reason why Nick, Jeff, Drew and Justin were thrilled to record that song for the "Mulan" soundtrack — they got to sing with the one and only legendary:
a) Bruce Springsteen
b) Billy Joel
c) Ray Charles
d) Stevie Wonder

15. Jeff is pretty close to perfect. (He's charming, sweet, intelligent, hot...) But he admits he's got one flaw (hard to believe, huh?). He:
a) bites his nails
b) twirls his thumbs
c) snores
d) cracks his knuckles

You call yourself a 98° fan? You think you're the only person on this planet who knows everything (and we mean everything!) about Nick, Justin, Drew, and Jeff? Yeah, we've heard that one before. So to test your 98° knowledge, we've devised a quiz to find out if you are truly, absolutely their biggest fan around.

1. Okay, we'll start this off easy to get you warmed up. What was the name of the second album the boys released?
a) "98° and Rising"
b) "Are You Feeling Hot, Hot, Hot?"
c) "Feelin' Sweaty"
d) "Holy Hot Tamale!"

2. Not only do Jeff, Nick, Justin, and Drew admire this group, but a record executive at their concert also discovered them. The group is:
a) Boyz II Men
b) Jodeci
c) Aerosmith
d) Metallica

3. Answer this: What's the name of the song they sang for the record exec at the concert?
a) "Blue Moon"
b) "In The Still of the Night"
c) "Stay"
d) "Amazed"

87

Test Your 98° I.Q.

By Geri Sahn

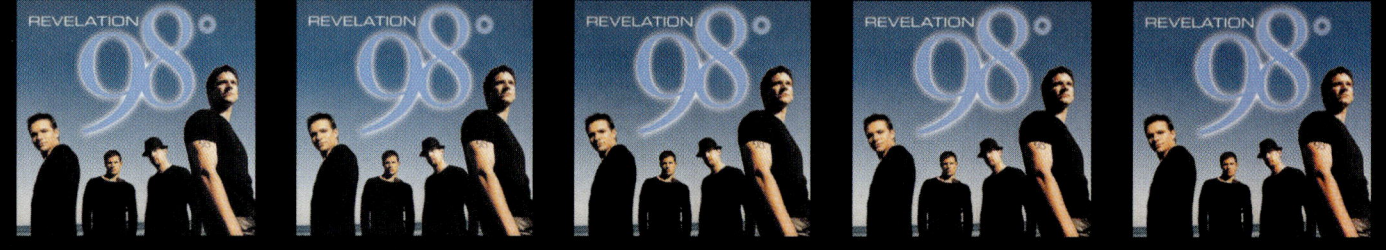

ALBUM NAME:
This Christmas
LABEL: Universal Records
RELEASED: Oct. 19, 1999

TRACKS:
1. If Every Day Could Be Christmas
2. God Rest Ye Merry Gentlemen
3. The Christmas Song (Chestnuts Roasting On An Open Fire)
4. I'll Be Home For Christmas
5. Oh Holy Night
6. This Gift
7. Little Drummer Boy
8. Christmas Wish
9. Silent Night
10. Ave Maria
11. This Gift (Pop Version)

QUICK ALBUM FACTS:
• 98°'s a cappella rendition of "I'll Be home For Christmas" was one of the songs the guys had recorded for their original demo tape.
• The album was certified platinum (1 million copies sold) on Dec. 29, 1999. It peaked at No. 27 on the Billboard Hot 200 album chart.

ALBUM NAME: Revelation
LABEL: Universal Records
RELEASE: Scheduled for Sept. 26, 2000
FIRST SINGLE: Give Me Just One Night (Una Noche)

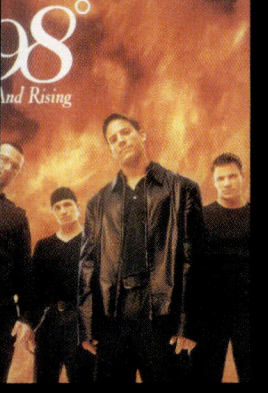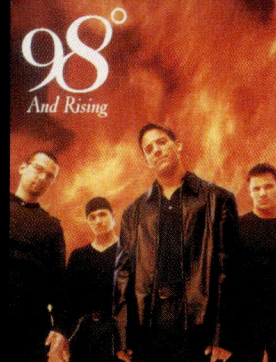

98° DISCOGRAPHY

Take a closer look at the music 98° has released leading up to its fantastic new album, "Revelation."

ALBUM NAME: 98°
LABEL: Motown Records
RELEASED: July 29, 1997
REISSUED: March 10, 1998

TRACKS:
1. Intro
2. Come And Get It
3. Invisible Man
4. Was It Something I Didn't Say
5. Take My Breath Away
6. Hand In Hand
7. Intermood
8. Dreaming
9. Heaven's Missing An Angel
10. I Wasn't Over You
11. Completely
12. Don't Stop The Love
13. I Wanna Love You

QUICK ALBUM FACTS:
- The album was re-released in March of 1998, with "Was It Something I Didn't Say," written by Diane Warren, replacing "You Are Everything."
- The single "Invisible Man" reached No. 12 on the Billboard Hot 100 chart.
- The album was certified gold (500,000 copies sold) on Oct. 22, 1997.

ALBUM NAME: 98° And Rising
LABEL: Motown Records
RELEASED: Oct. 27, 1998

TRACKS:
1. Intro
2. Heat It Up
3. If She Only Knew
4. I Do (Cherish You)
5. Fly With Me
6. Still
7. Because Of You
8. Give It Up - Interlude
9. Do You Wanna Dance
10. True To Your Heart
11. To Me You're Everything
12. The Hardest Thing
13. She's Out Of My Life

QUICK ALBUM FACTS:
- 98° helped write and/or produce nine of the tracks on this album.
- The single "Because Of You" reached No. 3 on the Billboard Hot 100 chart, and "The Hardest Thing" reached No. 5.
- The song "True To Your Heart" also appears in the animated motion picture "Mulan."
- The album was certified 4x platinum (4 million copies sold) on Jan. 27, 2000.

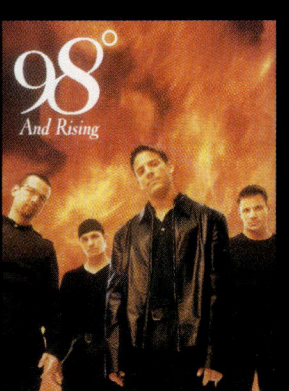

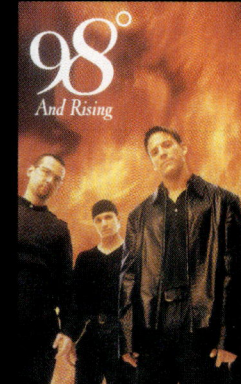

44) ODD MAN OUT

Originally, there was another member of 98° named Jonathan Lippman. He quit the group because he wanted to pursue acting instead. Maybe he should have stuck around, since the rest of the guys ended up signing a record deal just a few months after he signed off.

45) PATRIOT GAMES

The boys consider singing the national anthem before their hometown baseball team, the Cincinnati Reds, to be the highlight of their careers.

46) ONE SINGULAR SENSATION

98° doesn't really like being compared to other popular "boy bands." The members consider their sound and image unique and pride themselves on the fact that they were not manufactured by a record company.

47) GRIDIRON GREATS

One of Jeff's happiest childhood memories was getting to meet football legends Joe Namath and Roger Staubach.

48) HITTIN' THE SKINS

Drew plays the drums and other assorted percussion instruments.

49) TKO

Oops! Drew once socked Jeff in the face on-stage during a performance. Luckily, Jeff forgave his bud for the accidental sucker punch.

50) 98°... BELOW ZERO!

The video for "Invisible Man" was filmed at an old abandoned chemical factory in Long Island. Not only was the place filthy, it was also freezing cold!

26) BE ALL THAT YOU CAN BE
Jeff appeared in a commercial for the U.S. Navy. Ironically, it was his buddy, Drew, who actually enlisted in the Army once!

27) A BUG'S LIFE
Drew likes girls that aren't afraid of insects and other creepy-crawly critters. His girl has got to be cool with camping, too.

28) NICK'S PICKS
Nick's favorite singer is obviously Jessica Simpson, but he also admires the lovely Toni Braxton.

29) SOAP DISH
The group has made cameo appearances on the soaps "General Hospital" and "As The World Turns."

30) ASIAN APPEAL
Justin says his favorite touring destination was Indonesia because he says the fans there were wild and crazy.

31) PET PROJECT
The craziest gift the boys say they have ever received from a fan were tiny pet turtles. Unfortunately, the guys couldn't keep them because the mini-reptiles never would have survived on the road.

32) TWO LEFT FEET
Jeff admits that he's a total klutz and says he's the worst dancer of the bunch.

33) THE WRITE STUFF
All four of the guys write and produce the band's material.

34) FABULOUS FOUR EYES
Ever wonder why Justin is rarely seen without his shades? He hides those precious baby blues because he's always been a little shy. Now, fans give Justin sunglasses as gifts.

35) FLASH DANCE
Once, Nick's pants fell down on stage. Luckily, he grabbed them before he could reveal any incriminating anatomy. He managed to hold his trousers up with one hand for the rest of the song.

36) SPECIAL DELIVERY
Before making it big, Nick delivered Chinese food in Los Angeles. Once on his delivery route, he serenaded a beautiful girl, singing "In the Still of the Night." Too bad he "still" didn't manage to get her number!

37) HEY, BIG SPENDER!
Nick paid off college loans with his first 98° paycheck.

38) HEAD OF THE CLASS
Before joining the group, Justin wanted to become a history teacher.

39) THE NAME GAME
Before deciding on the name 98°, the guys had considered choosing these other names: Inertia, Next Issue and Verse Four. (Originally, they went by the name Just Us.)

40) UP ON THE ROOF
When the guys first came to L.A., they once climbed onto the roof of a parking garage. From this vantage point, they could watch their music idols arriving at the Grammy Awards ceremony, which was happening across the street. Little did they know they could end up performing at the Grammys one day!

41) SCHOOL DAYS
Jeff studied psychology in college, and Nick studied sports medicine.

42) SAFE KEEPING
Two bodyguards always accompany the band members on tour.

43) MATTERS OF THE HEART
Jeff was once said to be romantically linked to Mariah Carey. (He denies the claim, but says he wishes it were true!) All four guys admit they don't have much time for serious dating because they're too busy with their music.

13) ROAD HAZARD
Jeff failed his driving test the first time around.

14) LUCKY LADIES
The quartet hand-picks all the beautiful models, such as Ali Landry, who appear in their music videos.

15) BELLE OF THE BALL
The guys once took a lucky contest winner and three of her friends to her high school prom.

16) SCOT'S HONOR
Justin and Drew both love the movie "Braveheart."

17) WHERE CREDIT'S DUE
The band says they were inspired by the R&B group Boys II Men.

18) JUST "DREW" IT
Even though his real name is Andrew, don't call Drew Andy! He hates it.

19) BARE SKIN
Justin is the only band member who doesn't sport any tattoos. Why? First, he doesn't know what image he'd choose, and secondly, he hates needles!

20) WHAT'S IN A NAME?
Jeff's nickname is "Sugar." Justin's is "Droopy." Nick goes by "Hollywood," and Drew is called "Sprout."

21) GOT GAME?
The boys are addicted to sports – especially football. They could watch ESPN for hours, they say. They're particularly loyal to their Cincinnati sports teams, like the baseball Reds and the football Bengals.

22) BASHFUL BOY
Jeff says he still gets shy about asking girls out, although he admits to having a crush on Jennifer Lopez.

23) BODY LANGUAGE
The Japanese tattoos seen on Jeff's chest mean "heaven" and "good luck."

24) RAIN KING
Drew's favorite song is Prince's classic, "Purple Rain."

25) OLD SOUL
Even though he's the youngest member of the group, Drew is regarded by the other guys as a wise father figure.

FIFTY FAST FACTS 98°

GET THE 411 RIGHT HERE ON JUSTIN JEFFRE, JEFF TIMMONS AND NICK AND DREW LACHEY.

BY AMY HELMES

1) BODY ART
Brothers Nick and Drew both have the letter "L" tattooed in a band around their upper arms. The "L" stands for their last name, Lachey.

2) EATING HUMBLE PIE
Is there anything these talented cuties can't do? According to the guys, they could use a few more choreography lessons. They readily admit they're not the greatest dancers who ever graced a stage.

3) BRUSH OFF
Hats are Drew's trademark, mainly because he hates fussing with his hair.

4) QUICK CHANGE ARTISTS
During their most recent stage show, the guys change costumes five different times.

5) THE SPIRIT MOVED THEM
All the guys grew up singing in church. To this day, they say a group prayer before each performance.

6) PUCKER UP!
What is Justin's most prized possession? His trombone.

7) DRESSED TO THRILL
Jeff and Nick always love to wear funky, hip-hop-inspired clothing by Phat Farm.

8) OF MICE AND MEN
Not even Stuart Little could melt Drew's heart. He really HATES rodents.

9) LUCKY CHARMS
Jeff says he doesn't go anywhere without wearing his cross pendant necklace.

10) GREATEST AMERICAN HERO
Thanks to his Army medical training, Drew once saved a woman's life on an airplane.

11) HOMETOWN ZERO?
Believe it or not, the pop radio stations in Cincinnati (the boys' home base) were supposedly among the last to start playing 98° songs.

12) BEACHED BOY
Perhaps he's watched "Jaws" one time too many. In any case, Nick is deathly afraid of sharks and therefore won't venture too deep into the ocean.

98° BOULEVARD

http://degrees.if-only.net/

Webmaster Lena Soeung

Bathed in black, gray and blue, this ultra-organized site features a hefty photo gallery (including pics of the guys from childhood, Jeff at prom and shots from TRL and live performances), frequently updated news and a comprehensive archive of 98°' past interviews, articles and online chats.

The 17-year-old Webmaster has been a fan of 98° since 1997, when she first heard their song "Invisible Man," on a car ride home – and mistook them for Boys II Men.

When she became a fan, she was pleased to find the radio harmonies were coming from such delicious babes.

The 98° Boulevard site has a comprehensive news page that's updated frequently.

"The next time I went to a record store, I bought the album," Lena Soeung said. "That was also the first time I saw what they looked like. I was kind of surprised!"

A year later, when she was learning html, Soeung launched her fan site, 98° Boulevard. Designing the site from her home in Maine using several Web design and image programs, Soeung's initial plan for the site was to be a 98° free-for-all, Soeung said.

"I put just about everything I knew on them on the site," she said. "But I also put on stuff that I would want to know about the artist like schedules, appearances, news and things for the fans to do. It's a fan site, so I didn't just want information. I added E-Pals (the site's E-mail pen pal list) a few months back."

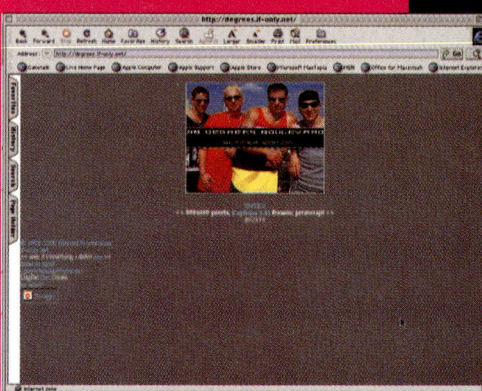

The site's index page

Fans have provided much of the news content, with Soeung filling in the rest from news and music sites, including 98°'s official site. Pictures come mostly from teen magazines.

Offline, the closest Soeung's gotten to the guys is about 15 feet, when they were in town for a private ticket-only radio concert in 1999. Still, she continues to praise the group on her Web site, which takes up much of her free time.

"(Updating the site) is a two-way job," said Soeung, who describes running the site as a second job (her first is finishing high school). "Sometimes I feel like I just post it and (other fans) provide the info with me as editor."

Splitting time between being a Webmaster and a fan isn't easy for enthusiasts of this busy vocal group. There's always new news, new pictures, new info to post.

But it can give the greatest of all fan fixes: Sharing online love for 98° with people across the globe. Now that's hot.

OTHER NOTABLES

The 98° Center
http://tinpan.fortunecity.com/eltonjohn/3/

Still 98°
http://still98.cjb.net/

The official 98° site
http://www.98degrees.com/

98° Burning Hot Heaven
http://www.angelfire.com/on2/98degreesburninghot/

98°: KEEP IT HOT AND STEAMY

http://kiss.to/hotsteamy98

Webmaster Diane Abundabar

This scandalously titled site is run by Diane Abundabar, 22, a senior at California State University, Chico. She's been a fan since 1997 ("Invisible Man" hooked her in.) She's met the guys twice – once at a hotel and once at a Japanese steakhouse – and gotten an autograph (nabbed by her boyfriend when she was sick in 1997.)

So when Webmaster met Web subject matter, did she tell them about her site? Nope, Abundabar says. She was too excited to even think of it. But the personal experience stories section (added in April 1999) remains her favorite part of the site.

Launched in early 1998 as a Backstreet Boys/98° fan base, the site was originally called "HOTTIES." But in October 1998, the Backstreet Boys were shown the back door and the site was officially redesigned as an all-access, all-98° site called "98°: Keep it Hot and Steamy."

"I just wanted to make a place on the Web that was mature and manifested the heat that 98° creates with their music," Abundabar said. "At first it was just a info and pics page. But after I met them, I put up live pictures and my experience story."

The site's content at first came courtesy of other 98° fan site Webmasters and magazines. Abundabar eventually added concert pics, a message board, mailing list and other areas to the site. As the site grew, she switched from hand-coding on her PC to using Web programs to cut time.

Although updates have slowed down, Abundabar is gearing up to cover the release of their new album.

"The guys have been low-key lately," she said.

Abundabar cites her Yahoo connection for providing the more than 100,000 hits she's gotten since starting the site.

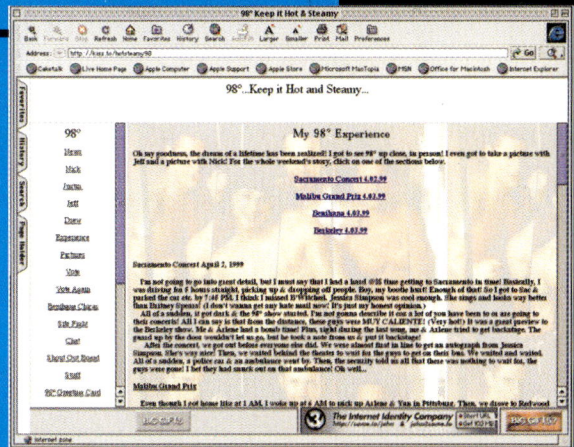

Abundabar says the most popular part of her site is the personal experience section.

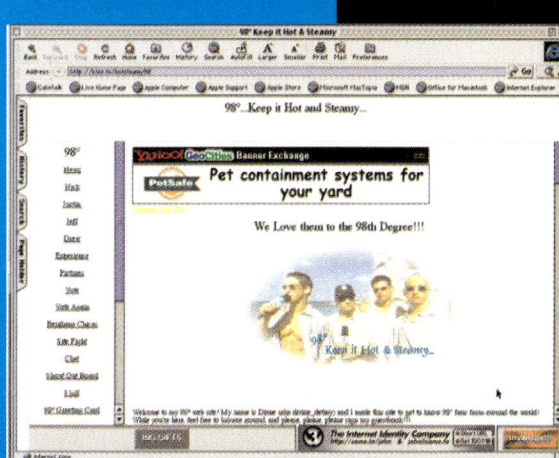

The site's index page

Other sites by this Webmaster

C Note: Can't Wait 'Til They Get Home
http://kiss.to/cnote

Back Here...With BBMak
http://bbmak.issexy.com/

BBMak Official Street Team
http://www.geocities.com/bbmakstreetteam/

Backstreet Boys: Hotties!
http://move.to/hotties

98° AND RISING
http://www.geocities.com/SunsetStrip/Frontrow/4750/

Unlike most fan sites, which feature extensive information about the site owner and his/her love for the site's subject, the 17-year-old Webmaster of 98° and Rising reveals only that she is from Canada and her name is Tracy (no last name is given on the site, nor did she divulge it in the interview).

There are no photos of Tracy on the site because her parents won't let her post pictures of herself on the Internet ("It's an issue with my parents," she said.) All she clues in about herself is that she has a yellow Labrador retriever, loves chocolate and wants to be a journalist when she grows up, or "possibly the editor of 'People' magazine."

Info on the site's Webmaster may be hazy, but the site's chock full of 98° background. A scrolling box on the left side of the screen updates users on the latest 98° news and rumors, and the site also includes downloadable screen savers, a tour dates list, info on upcoming and past TV appearances, a 98° newsletter, a "Shrines" section that showcases fan's 98°-coated rooms, a quiz, a message board to give a shout out to 98°, 98° e-postcards and more.

But the site's got more than just digital goodies: According to Stacy, it's got official 98° approval. When Stacy got a chance to meet the boys during a live radio appearance in Canada last year, to her surprise, Jeff told her he had visited her Web site before.

"98° are very down-to-earth guys who don't think of themselves as famous people," Stacy said of the meeting.

The 98° and Rising site is one of the oldest 98° sites on the Web, clocking in at four years (and counting). When Tracy began the site, she says she chose the name "to have something to do with the temperature rising and heat…it represents how HOT the group is!"

Early content was standard.

" Every fan site has to have the basics: News, bios, lyrics, pics, etc.," Stacy said. "I started out with the basics and then expanded it beyond what everyone else had. I added sections for trading, rumors, cool facts, clones, shrines, TV appearances, fans helping fans and tons more."

Tracy still uses the official 98° site for news and tour dates, but much of her site's news comes from magazines and other fans. The site is updated biweekly (sometimes weekly) during big news times, and Tracy spends about 45 to 60 minutes a day answering site E-mails.

"Any musical fan site takes a lot of work because you constantly need to update it with new single releases, pics, tour dates and lyrics," Tracy said. "Lyrics are the worst when artists release new albums because everyone immediately wants lyrics."

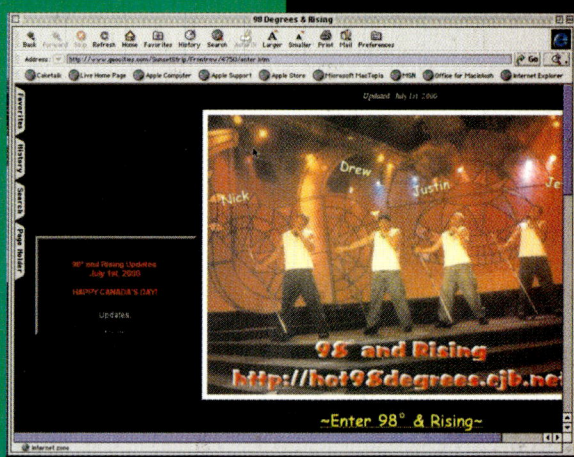

The index page of 98° and Rising features scrolling news headlines.

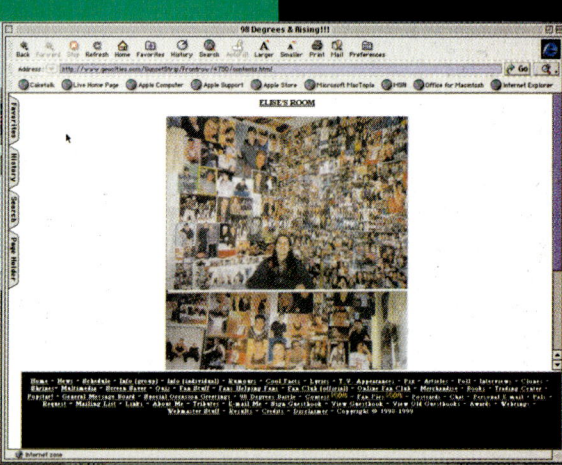

The site's "Shrines" section offers a glimpse at the poster-covered bedrooms of super 98° fans.

Other sites by this Webmaster

Westlife Online
http://westlifeonline.cjb.net/

5ive Bad Boyz
http://5ivebadboyz.cjb.net/

*N Luv With Justin Timberlake
http://members.tripod.com/JustinsAngel/

Sites for Sore Eyes

Wading through the sea of fan sites for a good 98°
homebase? Check out these tributes.